Bound by a Common Thread

Memoirs of people living in the backwoods of Maine

by **Charlie Reitze**

Leicester Bay
B O O K S

Newport, Maine

Prepared by
Leicester Bay Books
Newport, Maine
www.leicesterbaybooks.com

2019 Print Version
ISBN-13: 9781793392671
2019 Kindle Version also available

The photos of Charlie Reitze on the cover and *About The Author* page were taken by Judyth B. Reitze at the Chain of Ponds in western Maine.

OTHER BOOKS BY CHARLIE REITZE
(from Leicester Bay Books):

Grampa Charlie's Side-splittin' Fireside Stories
For bed time or any other time at all

A forthcoming book: **SURVIVAL!**

CONTENTS

Acknowledgements

Prolog

Dedication

Introduction 1

1–*On Holeb Pond:* The Last of a Breed 13

2–*Dawn At Roque Bluffs:* Living Our Dream 29

3–*Mountain Pond:* Interlude 41

4–*Solon:* Creep City 45

5–*Grand Isle:* Rose 69

6–*On The Canadian Border:* Spirit and Faith 87

7–*Grand Lake Matagamon:* The Guides 103

8–*Monson:* Oak Mountain Lodge 121

9–*Chesuncook Lake:* The Lost Village 137

10–*Waldoboro:* The Mysterious Stranger 159

11–*Chain of Ponds:* Generations 175

12–*Linneus:* It's Home 181

Epilogue 201

About The Author 206

Acknowledgements

No writer completes a project like this without help. I owe a great debt to my sister Kathy Lewia for the long hours she spent critiquing my first drafts, to my sister Sue McKinley for helping transcribe some of my tapes, and to Sue Kinnie who also transcribed many tapes. I wish to thank Claire Nelson of the University of Maine at Farmington who helped me get started in college, Lee Sharkey who assisted me far and beyond any of her college responsibilities, Wesley McNair for taking me on as a directed-study student - for his long hours and honest criticism, Bill Roorbach who taught me how to write my book as a cohesive unit, and Pat O'Donnell whose class in contemporary literature taught me a great deal about diction and style. Wes once jokingly told Pat, "Don't get involved in Charlie's writing; he'll bury you in manuscripts."

The obsession Wes remarked about has at long last led to this book. In the pages that follow, I welcome you to my world of the people who live in the backwoods of Maine.

Prolog

The title of this book came to me while I was returning home from visiting one of the protagonists who appear within its pages. While driving down Interstate 95, deep in thought about what the title should be, I distinctly remember hearing the words *Bound By A Common Thread* come to my mind. They came with such clarity that I immediately pulled over so that I could write what I heard. Even the conclusion which until now had been so elusive was revealed to me.

Now that may sound crazy to some but at the same time it will ring true to many others. As Tom Brown once said, "There is a spirit that moves in all things." On at least two occasions that same spirit saved my life in Vietnam. And I will always believe that it was guiding my footsteps throughout this book. One of my professors called it serendipity.

"**What**?" I asked out loud as I pulled over. I grabbed my pen and a small note book off of the dashboard and immediately started writing; I didn't want to miss anything that came to my mind. If you ignore those kinds of promptings, inner thoughts, you are left feeling that you forgot an important dream that you wished you had written down when you first woke up.

"Yes," I thought, as I sat there frantically writing, not wanting to miss any thoughts that were flooding my mind. "Each of these people has a common thread or lifestyle that links them together. They have found peace in living close to the earth, and each, in his (or her) own way, has shared that peace with me."

Dedication

I dedicate this book to all those who have so richly blessed my life and helped me heal from the wounds of Vietnam, specifically:

To the "Spirit that moves in all things," the same Spirit who continues to guide me;

To my sweet, gentle, kind, loving, huggable, teddy-bear, wife, Judy Barton, who is my sweetheart, my eternal companion, who always comforts and consoles me when my heart is heavy;

To those who choose to live off the blacktop, off the grid, who live where they have to paddle eighteen miles, or walk two miles through mosquito-infested swale, to get to their homes – and who, through their gracious and gentle living helped me find my life;

To my father, Raymond E. Reitze, Sr., who was captured during World War II by Rommel at Kasserine Pass in North Africa, and who spent twenty-six months as a POW in German Stalags;

To my sweet mother, Mary J. Reitze, who served on the home-front by welding ships at the shipyard at Portland, Maine;

To my brother, Raymond E. Reitze Jr., who served in Vietnam the year before I did;

To my nephew, Scott McKinley, who served in Iraq;

To all the soldiers who have served their country with honor, who are now serving, and who will yet serve;

To these great men, women, their families all across America, and to all those who gave their all, I dedicate this book.

May God bless each of you.

Introduction

"There are some who can live without wild things, and some who cannot," Aldo Leopold wrote in his foreword to *A Sand County Almanac*.

I – am someone who cannot. I find peace and contentment away from the flashing lights – away from the backbiting, picketing, radio-blaring, left and right wing pandemonium of twentieth and twenty-first century America. Beyond all this confusion, there is a way of life in the woods of Maine that is as relaxing and unwinding as the people who live in it.

Growing up in Buxton, Maine, about fifteen miles west of Portland, I always dreamed of living in the backwoods away from towns and cities. At my dad's camp in Eustis, I dreamed about being a forest ranger, trapper, hunter, camper, fisherman, and mountain man. I thought I was alone in those dreams. As I grew older, I discovered that most, if not all, kids at one time or another have their own youthful dreams.

Yet my dreams went much deeper than most; I lived my dreams. While my eighth grade class went to a museum in Boston, I went with my parents to their log camp in Eustis, Maine. While other boys and girls were dating, I was hunting rabbits, partridge, deer, and bear. In the summer time and during high school vacations when I wasn't milking cows, haying, and feeding chickens, I jumped in my '61 Comet and took off to Eustis. On scheduled dates, my parents would meet me at their camp on Dead River. I'd prepare a trout feed for them, and then be off to Snow Mountain Pond, the Chain of Ponds, Jim Pond, Bugeye

Pond, or some other body of water to catch some more. From Eustis to Rangeley, to North New Portland, to Coburn Gore, to Jackman, to the northern village of Allagash, I knew the geography of northern and western Maine. There wasn't much of it that I hadn't traveled. In my wanderings, I made friends with many people who sought out the same solitude, who lived in the backcountry — and many still do.

(Charlie in uniform at Fort Leonard Wood Missouri.)

In 1967 after graduating from Bonny Eagle High School in Standish, Maine, I joined the Army. In September of

1968, my life turned upside down. I found myself in the hellish, blood-stained soils of Vietnam. No longer could I go to camp. No longer could I go fishing. No longer could I do the things that I so much loved. Instead of camping in a tent on some remote pond, I now lived in shoebox-like tin barracks and sandbag bunkers. Instead of carrying a fishing pole, I carried an M-16. And even though I was thousands of miles from home as opposed to hundreds of miles, in my yearning for the woods I loved so much, I'd often hum the song – quite pensively, *"five hundred miles, five hundred miles, five hundred miles away from home, oh, I'm five hundred miles away from home. Away from home, away from home, I'm . . . five . . .* **'Thousand'** *. . . miles . . . away from . . . home."*

I spent the most terror-filled, horrifying, life-altering year of my life in that war-torn nation. I didn't know it then, but when my physical self returned home, my jovial self never would. War forever scars a man. He is never the same; nor will he ever be. Somewhere, buried in the blood-stained soils of every war-torn battle field, every soldier leaves part of himself forever behind. He returns distant, detached, and aloof. His friends don't know him, because he won't let himself get close to them. His family longs for the son or sibling who used to be – and so does he.

Just before I went to Vietnam, my company went to Germany from Fort Dix, New Jersey. I ended up in the army hospital at Fort Dix with back issues. When I was released from the hospital, I had orders for Vietnam. I was an engineer trained at Fort Leonard Wood, Missouri as a crane and shovel operator. When I arrived at the 62nd Engineer Battalion in Long Bien, Vietnam, they didn't have a crane, so they put me in a supply room and taught me to be a weapons expert.

(Charlie with an M-60 by the Supply Room)

Their weapons specialist had gone home and they needed another — so they trained me. Once I had learned how to repair, and in some cases rebuild, various weapons, from M-60 machine guns, M-79 grenade launchers, M-16 and M-14 rifles, they taught me how to drive a ten-ton tractor trailer and sent me out on convoys. When we returned from convoys, I repaired weapons. I even built my own M-16 from spare parts. In order to do it, I had to steal the serial-numbered item from the weapons dump, only to have a new CO, Captain Peters, come in and take it away from me. Captain Peters didn't believe I had built it and told me when he found out where I got it, he was going to send me to LBJ, that is, Long Bien Jail. Needless to say, I never went to jail.

We drove all-wheel-drive ten-ton trucks with flatbed trailers and hauled jungle-mauling bulldozers with Rome Plows and various types of ammo. Some times we drove with our tractor roofs down and the windshields lying on the hoods so we'd have a better field of fire. On some convoys, in hot areas, we were escorted by tanks, apc's (armored personal carriers), and the infantry. When we got to where we were going, we'd offload the dozers and clear large areas of jungle. When we left an area, the infantry, or some other outfit, would take over, and we'd be off on another mission. When a dozer hit a mine, it would blow the track right off of it. When a truck hit a mine, it blew shrapnel right up through the floor boards. Injured dozer operators and drivers were medevaced out by choppers.

(Ten-Ton Tractor Blown Up by a Land Mine)

Most nights in the dry season, the safest place to sleep was on the ground under our flatbed trailers. In the monsoon season, we slept in our cabs.

During the '68/'69 Tet Offensive, we were overrun at

Long Bien; 122mm rockets rained death from the sky. One sergeant and two other soldiers in our company were killed that night. Another soldier was reduced to nothing more than a vegetable. During the attack as I ran for a bunker, I found myself lying on my face in the dirt. My mind was all fuzzy; I had no idea what happened. I was rattled and shaken. As I recall, when the cobwebs cleared, I knew that a rocket had landed far enough away so that it didn't kill me, but close enough to blow me off my feet. I didn't seem to have any strength and my knees were gashed and bleeding, not so much from shrapnel as I later determined, but from the fall. Nowhere was it safe. All anyone could do was pray and hope that a rocket didn't land any closer than the concussion from the one that had already taken me down. Some men were hiding under the mattresses in their shoebox-like tin-can barracks, while others were running for the safety of bunkers. There were both screams of fist-pounding, murderous rage as three men fell, and yet, somehow, there was a terror-filled, eerie silence that seemed to penetrate the night. It was a gut wrenching fear. This was hell on earth. It was real. It was war.

The rioting, picketing, spitting, pot-smoking, non-inhaling hippies back home could call it anything they wanted. But to us, to the soldiers in Vietnam – to those who were man enough to fight for their country, it was a blood-curdling nightmare. The worst part was that we had two wars to fight – the one in Vietnam and the one back home against those protesting, pot-smoking hippies, hippies that had no idea where their freedom came from, much less care. We did. We were fighting Communism. We were fighting so the South Vietnamese could enjoy the same freedom that allowed the thoughtless, mindless protesters back home to scream and holler, and picket.

During the Tet Offensive, as I laid with my face pressed into the blood-stained soil, many things passed through my mind. I believed that, at the young age of nineteen, my life was over. My throbbing head and bloodied, aching knees told me that I was still alive. But I didn't seem to have any strength. My limbs were like rubber. I had fallen hard, and wondered how a rocket could land so close without killing me. My whole life passed like a movie through my mind – "The Good, The Bad, and The Ugly. [That's a Clint Eastwood movie.]

I still remember looking heavenward and praying. It was the first time I had ever uttered a heartfelt prayer. "Heavenly Father," I prayed, "if you let me live through this night, let me survive Vietnam, I'll go to church the rest of my life." Though at the time, I didn't understand the depth of my promise, a loving Heavenly Father did. And when I came home, he set me on a path that would allow me to fulfill it.

"I'll go to church the rest of my life," I repeated. "Let me see my girl friend one more time, my mother, my father, my brother one more time. Let me see my sisters one more time. Let me see my friends one more time." As I laid there praying, somehow, I could feel my strength slowly returning.

I wept and rose to a crouching position and wondered how badly I was hurt. I hobbled to the closest bunker. For the next three days, I couldn't eat or drink. Nothing would stay down. My nerves were completely rattled. But in times like that as difficult as it is, you have to keep your wits about you. You can't panic or you'll be useless to yourself and dangerous to those around you. Every soldier depends on every other to stay alive. So we all did what we had to do. But, the Vietcong had overrun our perimeters. In spite of our own efforts, we never would have made it through that night if it hadn't been for the Hueys, (attack helicopters). They rained their own death from the sky. Tracer rounds lit up the sky. It looked like 100 Fourth of July's all wrapped up in one. For those of us on the ground, it was a life-saving sight. We all felt a great relief. You could almost feel the tension ease; actually – you could.

(Gunships like this saved our lives during the Tet Offensive.)

•••••

When I processed out of the Army in 1970, I went to camp. I went to Snow Mountain Pond. I went to all of my old places. I camped, tented, and fished. Often I went alone. I found places where I could cry if I wanted to cry, places where the reawakened fantasies of my childhood began to salve the wounds of Vietnam. I'd camp for a week or two at a time. I needed to be clean and free. I'd strip naked and swim in the lakes, streams, and ponds – and so felt cleansed from the blood of a corrupted soil and free to establish my life once again. Physically, I was home; psychologically, part of me would always be in Vietnam. And though I didn't know it then, later I realized that none of us who served in war, any war, would ever be the same. Personalities change forever.

Finally, on one hot summer day as I paddled carefree in my cedar strip canoe on the calm waters of Baker Pond, up by Eustis, things seemed to change. I lived a dream deeper than any I had ever known. I felt as if I were in my childhood once more, reborn in the country I had loved ever since I could remember. My thoughts drifted back to Southeast Asia. Somehow I finally understood that it was possible to let go of the baggage I carried from Vietnam, at least a lot of it. I knew that until I did let it go, I would never be free. The only battles that faced me now were the ones within me. At that moment, I paddled my way from the past into the future.

My thoughts also drifted back to various people I had met in the woods over the years, people who lived the life that I was seeking. Thinking about how relaxed and happy they always were, I wondered if writing about them might help me find peace as well.

I decided to pursue a degree in writing at the University of Maine at Farmington, a college that borders the western mountains of Maine. My principal writing subject became the people who lived in the woods. For the next three years, I traveled the state looking for them, taping conversations and furiously taking notes. I spent my time between classes transcribing, writing, rewriting – thinking through my fingertips.

I established certain criteria for the people I would interview.

- They had to live off the grid.
- They had to understand what it meant to be alone, what it meant to be close to the earth.
- Instead of electricity, they had to rely on kerosene, gas, candles, or a generator.
- They couldn't have running water.
- They had to use a hand pump, a bucket, and an outhouse.
- They had to walk, ride horseback, snowshoe, canoe, or snowmobile to their houses.
- In the absence of a nearby hospital, they had to rely on home remedies, midwives, or Dad's nervous fingers on a slippery new baby.

I wanted people who understood what it meant to live *"THE GOOD LIFE."*

To meet these people, I lived out of "Festus," my Toyota truck, and a leaky tent. I roamed the state of Maine three times. I snowshoed across Grand Lake Matagamon. I rode a snowmobile along the mountainous roads of Coburn Gore. I canoed eighteen miles up Chesuncook Lake. I hiked the mountains of Monson. I was backed up to one man's front door by a vicious dog in Waldoboro. I walked two miles through mosquito-infested swale in Roque Bluffs. I slept on a roofed picnic table during a violent thunderstorm at Chemquasabamticook Lake (Ross Lake).

(Tenting on a Picnic Table on the way to Oak Mountain)

I found the people I was looking for – and found myself in the process.

(Charlie Searching)

Chapter One
On Holeb Pond
The Last of a Breed

The clothesline rope twisted and tightened. Allan Szarka, my ruddy-faced, scruffy-bearded college friend from Jackman, pulled the rope over his canoe, wrapped it around a hook on the passenger side of Festus, my Toyota pickup truck, and tugged on it as we tied the canoe down.

"I think Aime Lecours is just the kind of guy you're looking for," Allan hollered, as he tugged on a second rope that I had tossed over the canoe. "Aime lives alone on an island at Holeb Pond. The man's an old trapper and logger from way back. He only comes out of the woods twice a year — once at freeze up and once at spring thaw."

After securing the canoe, Allan walked over to his old Ford, leaned through the open window, and grabbed *The Maine Atlas*. He laid it across the hood of his truck and pointed out the winding roads that led to Aime's.

"You may be making a wasted trip," Allan said. "I don't know if Aime will even talk to you. He's refused to talk to anyone else who wanted to write about him. If you do get him talking, though, be prepared for a long sit. Once he starts talking, he never stops."

A few miles north of Allan's place in Jackman, I started down a dirt road toward Holeb Pond, a small body of water in Holeb Township only a few miles from the Canadian border and about fifteen miles from Jackman. The road threaded its way around sharp bends and over camel-hump hills. Festus bounced through mud puddles, wheel ruts and potholes, reminding me of the times I drove a ten-ton tractor on backcountry dirt roads in Vietnam. The roads were so rough that the stock on my M-14 rifle broke in half when it fell from the hook I had improvised to hang it on.

During the ride, I kept looking over my shoulder. I was jittery. My mind kept racing back in time. No matter how hard I tried to forget, the horrors of Southeast Asia persisted in invading my life. I was sweating and bouncing down this narrow, tree-lined, dirt memory. Fifteen miles and forty-five minutes later, I sat on the sandy shores of Holeb Pond, mentally exhausted with my head buried in my hands. I was shaking, trembling and wondering how many years it would take before I could live a normal life—or if...

Like many young Vietnam Veterans drinking was my way of life. I just kept trying to forget. But, the protesters kept protesting. The picketers kept picketing. The Tet Offensive was like watching a horror movie over and over. I drank so much Canadian Club and chased it with so much Budweiser that sometimes I wasn't worth a bucket of stove-wood ashes. I was lonely, longing for the Charlie that used to be. I longed to look down a dirt road and not see dead Vietcong piled in four-foot high rows with their blank hollow eyes staring back at me. Their black silky clothing, stained with dried blood, stank.

My mother kept at me to quit drinking. She pleaded, sometimes with tears in her eyes, "Charlie, when are you going to quit drinking?". She hurt to see me in such a state.

But it wasn't until 1972 when a loving Heavenly Father stepped into my life that I was able to quit my alcohol habit. I had forgotten my promise to Him in Vietnam to go to church the rest of my life, but Heavenly Father hadn't forgotten. Through a series of events, He reminded me of my promise. He brought the Gospel of Jesus Christ right to my doorstep. When my first wife investigated The Church of Jesus Christ of Latter-day Saints, I wasn't interested and refused to listen to the missionaries. Later, when she was having difficulties with the birth of our first child (he was two weeks overdue), I got on my knees for the first time since I left Vietnam. During that prayer, I promised Heavenly Father that if the child would be born healthy – and would be a boy – that I would finally listen to the missionaries. Within two hours after that prayer, she was in the hospital. After she came home from the hospital – with a healthy boy – she asked me if I would listen to the missionaries *NOW*. I told her, "I don't dare not to. I promised Heavenly Father that I would if the baby was born healthy." She called Bishop Garner in Portland and asked him to send the missionaries to visit us. After offering beers to the missionaries during dinner, I looked at them and asked, "So, if I am going to join your church I have to give up drinking, is that right?"

"Yes, that's right," said Elder Baker, a missionary from Calgary, Alberta, Canada.

"Then I'll quit," I said. "I believe the church is true."

"Do you want me to help you get rid of it?" Elder Baker, asked.

"No," I said, "If I'm going to do this, I have to do it myself."

Without another word, I went to the cupboard, grabbed three bottles of Canadian Club, went to the fridge and grabbed two six-packs of Budweiser, went to the bathroom to get three more six-packs, and then I went to the sink and turned out every last drop. That was the end of my drinking.

I went cold turkey that night.

And so, here I was standing on the sandy shores of this small pond with a half-mile of angry, windswept water between me and Birch Island. Then my thoughts turned to the island and getting there safely.

Backing the truck down the sandy beach, I remembered something Allan had said: "Aime is happily married, but has lived alone on the island for seven years. His wife Angelina lives in Jackman." As I stared across the choppy water, I kept trying to change my mind-set by imagining a man who was "happily married," care-taking cabins on a remote island while his wife lived in town — especially a man who was ninety years old. But according to Allan, this had been Aime's way-of-life since some game-warden friends told him that the people who owned the island would pay him a hundred dollars a week to look after their cabins.

I was excited but apprehensive about meeting Aime. I had no idea what kind of reception I'd get. I had no idea where exactly his camp was, or even if he was home. Kneeling in Allan's sixteen-foot Old Town canoe, I drove the paddle into the sandy shoreline, gave a giant heave, and shoved off toward the American flag flapping in the wind — tree-top high over the distant camps that lined the island's west end.

A little more than halfway across, black clouds rolled in bringing a stronger wind and churning up white, biting breakers that slammed into my canoe. It was too late to go back; the island was closer than the mainland shore. The west end, my destination, was now far to my right, and the nearest shore was quickly disappearing as the wind forced me to the east faster than I could compensate. I turned the canoe into the wind, trying to not overshoot the island's east end and trying to avoid getting swamped. At times the wind forced me backward more than I could paddle forward. After more than an hour of bucking, rolling, and frantic paddling, I dragged the canoe across the shoreline and collapsed on the beach.

After a short rest, I began searching the immediate camps. In quite a pleasant mood by now, singing Johnny Cash's song about a "dirty old egg-sucking dog," I jumped back in the canoe, and ducked in and out of coves checking each camp as I circled the island. An hour later, having worn out the song, I paddled the canoe up to the backside of the island and tied it to a rusty bedspring sticking out of a clump of alders. I climbed some ledges to check the last few cabins hoping I hadn't made a wasted trip.

Suddenly, I heard an unfamiliar French tune. It could only be coming from Aime Lecours. I spotted him through the trees with his back to me, hoeing in one of four newly planted gardens. He hung his hoe in a rack of moose antlers spiked to a tree and walked to the woodpile, grabbing a shiny double-bitted axe. Soon he was splitting a twelve-inch piece of hardwood with one hit – like a man in his twenties.

"Hello," I hollered, drawing into shouting range.

Aime turned fully around and walked toward me, carrying the axe in his right hand — an axe he knew how to use.

"Who are you?" he asked. I stared at that large axe, hoping he was friendly.

"I'm doing some writing in college and thought you might be able to give me some information I could use. Allan Szarka at Bishop's Store in Jackman told me how to find you," I said.

With one hand, Aime buried the knife-edge of his axe

two inches deep in a block of hardwood. "I can still keep up with you young fellers," he said, smiling. You say you're going to college? Well, I don't always talk to folks that want information, but it don't much matter anymore. Come on in the house an' set a spell. I don't get many visitors up in this country. Have any trouble gettin' to the island?"

"You bet I did," I replied. "The wind was blowing so hard, I came within ten feet of missing the island."

"The wind's most always blowin' hard out yonder," Aime said, as we stepped into the house. We sat in wooden-doweled chairs that were pulled up to a rectangular table stacked high with tools and paperwork. Aime's eyes were hidden behind a pair of black glasses, which I later learned were prescribed after a recent cataract operation. Aime ran a little to flab, his skin sagged down under his biceps where larger muscles used to be. He was about five-foot-seven or -eight inches tall, with sleek gray hair.

"Had a feller one night blown clean ta' the other end of the pond," Aime said as soon as we settled. "His motor conked out. I saw him flashin' his flashlight. Time I got to him, his boat was ruined. The wind smashed it to smithereens up again' the rocks."

Apart from the cluttered table, Aime kept his home quite neat for an old man living alone. His couch-bed was made and turned partway down, ready to climb into. The kitchen sink was empty, the counter clean, and the floors swept. But the small windows didn't allow much light in the cabin and when I asked if we could turn on a light, he said, "The mantles in my lights are broke."

"Well," I replied, "if you give me some mantles, I'll fix 'em for ya."

Chuckling, he said, "How do you s'pose I'm gonna find

any mantles in this heap? 'Sides that, I go to bed when the lights up yonder go out, or I'da fixed 'em myself."

He slid his chair back away from the table and walked to a kitchen sink that was made of black slate. He cupped his hands, scooped cold water out of a bucket, and then dipped his face into his hands. "I been washin' like this for years. It wakes a man up," he said through a chuckle.

Sitting back at the table, Aime began telling me his life story. He was born in Canada during tough economic times. The way he put it: "I was born very young, ya know, I think I was just nine months old."

Seeking a better life, his family moved to Richmond, Maine from Lac Megantic, Quebec in 1911. Aime was only eight years old. He was the eighth of what was to be twenty-two children. His father worked at a cotton mill in Richmond and later at a railroad car shop in Brunswick. On January 1, 1914, the family moved to Jackman. Later that month, Aime turned twelve.

His father and a brother both died at ninety-five. "I expect to live a spell yet," said the ninety-one-year-old Aime.

"Back when we were kids, we ate venison and baked taters year-round. We had no butter, no nothin'. Mother just fixed 'em different ways. We didn't have shoes, neither. We went barefoot all summer, and Mother made us moccasins out of burlap bags in the winter. It made us tough."

Getting up from the kitchen table, he motioned toward the door. We stepped off the front steps and into the garden. He leaned on his hoe and pointed out rows of recently planted potatoes, tomatoes, peppers, and other vegetables.

Aime explained that he hoes everything, using mostly compost from garbage, ashes, leaves, pine needles, and anything else he can find for fertilizer. "That's all I've ever needed," he said.

Bending over, picking up a handful of dirt and letting it sift through his fingers, Aime kept right on talking. "Look at that. Ain't it nice, rich soil? That's why I've got four gardens. I plant tomatoes in one, taters in another, and vegetables in the other two. Then, the folks on the island give me all kinds of food every time they leave camp to go home."

"I learned to work young. At age twelve, I worked at a sawmill in Jackman with my father. I worked so darn hard I stayed short," he said, laughing again at his own humor. He slapped his knee for emphasis.

"There wasn't anything on me very big. At age sixteen, I was only four feet tall. At age seventeen, I was the strongest man in Jackman. Work's good for people, but a lot don't believe it," Aime said. "I only weighed a hundred forty-eight pounds back in those days. But I had to give up sawmill work. The state passed a new law, and the mill let me go because I was too young to work. My father told them if I was too young, then he was too old. He quit."

Aime's personality had become readily apparent — he had a quick wit and an incessant need to talk. Every time I tried to speak, he held up his right index finger, motioning me to remain quiet. He spoke with pride about his gardens, the upkeep of the cabins, and his ability to live alone on an island despite days when the temperatures plunged to forty below. He was a man who was strong, independent, and, at the same time, terribly lonesome. I sat on an ancient stump by the edge of the garden and listened while he leaned on his hoe and continued telling his life story.

"Father always hooked moose and horses up together to haul wood," he said. "I can tell ya, it was quite a sight. But it was back when father quit the mill that I moved to Skinner. I lived where the south and west branches of Moose River meet, and I rented a camp for four dollars a month. The camp was a fifteen- to twenty-mile paddle west from here on Moose River. I had to take the train in there, too. I trapped to survive."

He pointed to some of his old traps hanging on the woodshed. He choked up a little, thinking of the old days. "There wasn't any work to be had. But the Farmington zoo was paying twenty-five dollars for young bear. I had one bear that was so friendly I led him around on a collar. I trapped bear and shipped them to the zoo, until a bear killed a tourist and the state put a stop to it."

"Ya know, I really like living like this. I don't smoke and I don't drink, so I don't need much money. There's no pressure and I'm mighty comfortable. It's just the way I choose to live," he said, rubbing his growling belly. "I useta smoke; I started smokin' a pipe in 1908, when I was six. I'd smoke in front of the fireplace, where Father couldn't smell it. When I was twelve, he gave me permission. Years later, I started spittin' black, and hearin' humming noises. I quit in 1937. I'm glad I did. It's a bad habit."

Aime doesn't trap bear anymore, but he still traps beaver, fox, and muskrat. He has also taken care of places like Boundary Pond Camps, Parlin Pond Camps, and he helped build Rock Pond Camps. When he wasn't working on the camps, he worked in the woods while his wife, Angelina, waitressed at some of the camps.

Aime lived alone in his rented camp until the 1920s when he married at the age of twenty-four. At thirty-four, he bought the camp for one hundred dollars. He and Angelina lived there for twenty-seven years.

In the 1980s, he moved to the island and Angelina

moved to Jackman. Aime was just 83.

Hanging the hoe he'd been leaning on for the last half-hour back in the fork of the antlers, Aime motioned for me to follow him. "Come with me," he said, "and I'll show ya around the island."

(Aviation Fuel Tank for Water Storage on Birch Island)

At one side of the garden, Aime hopped over a three-foot ledge like an agile young boy, talking as he went. "Years ago, the island was all white birch trees. As you can see, they've mostly all died. Now these spruce and fir cover most of it."

Aime kicked some dead pine limbs out of our way, broke off a couple of low-hanging branches for me, and then pointed through the trees. "There's the old cold-water storage tank. It's a seventeen-hundred-gallon aviation fuel tank. Water was pumped up from the pond by a generator. Afterward, it gravity-fed to a hotel and some of the other buildings. There's the old water line."

"Back before the crash in '29," he said, walking out of

the wooded area into the open, where the other buildings edge the pond, "a group of wealthy business people from Boston owned and ran the island's eighteen-room hotel. They had a separate dining hall, icehouse, and washhouse. All the buildings ran on electricity supplied by the generator."

(Old Birch Island Hotel)

Aime also showed me the old hotel, icehouse, and dining hall. A Bendix dryer, Lazy-Boy washing machine, and steam press were piled under a mountain of discarded junk inside the wash house. Looking at the press, I hollered to Aime as he stepped out the back door, "This must have been some operation."

"Yup, the early owners named the island Little Boston and called the hotel the Boston Ranch. During the crash they lost all their money and the island was later sold for a dollar." Aime put his right index finger to his head, as if aiming a gun, then clicked his tongue, saying, "Many of 'em shot themselves. Ain't that somethin', that money can mean all that?"

We walked over to the edge of the pond, where I had tied Allan's canoe, Aime pointed across the water. "That long flat area you see over there is the railroad bed. Back in the twenties there were no roads to Holeb. Everyone rode the passenger trains, then boated or canoed the half-mile to the island."

"Time for lunch," I interrupted, worn out from listening and following, and hungry from the long paddle.

Aime didn't hear. He couldn't stop talking.

He sat down on some ledges that overlooked the pond, crossed his legs like an old Indian, and grabbed a piece of grass to chew on between breaths. "The day trains were numbered thirty-nine, forty, forty-one, and forty-two. The night trains were numbered seventeen and eighteen. There was a train every three-quarters of an hour. Them trains ran from Brownville Junction to Montreal, and clean to St. John, New Brunswick. It was a busy place back then."

Aime pointed off to the west across the pond. "If I ever quit taking care of this island, I'm going back to Skinner. It's beautiful there. I always fed the chickadees when they landed on me while I was skinnin' beaver, and I had great fun talkin' to all the Gorby birds (Canadian Jays). You should hear them birds talk. I tell ya, it was comical. Back then I'd catch five-pound salmon, too. I don't fish anymore. The doctor told me not to lift anything over ten pounds. I hate to keep cutting my line, so I quit fishing."

He chuckled and shook his head.

The first summer Aime worked at Birch Island, he still lived in Skinner. Every day he walked a mile from his camp to the river, then paddled his ten-foot pram (a lightweight, flat-bottom boat) to the island. "I enjoyed the trip," Aime said, looking out across the pond, "comin' and goin'. I always saw lots of moose and deer. Most folks can only tell ya' what a river looks like goin' downstream. I can tell ya what it looks like goin' in either direction."

Wood smoke billowed out of the chimney as we walked back toward the cabin. Aime both cooked and heated with a Shenandoah woodstove. He burned fifteen cords of wood a year. Some of his wood came from the dead trees on the island, but most of it he dragged from the mainland across the ice using his pickup truck.

"Cuttin' wood is good exercise," he said and then excused himself to go to the outhouse. He kept right on talking once he got inside. "So's lugging my drinking water. I get it from a spring at Turner Pond. I haul my bath water up from this pond and heat it on the stove."

"Ouch!" I heard a loud slap. "Ya know, I freeze my butt off in this outhouse in the winter and the bugs chew it off in the summer. But at least my toilet don't plug up."

(Aime's Outhouse.)

He continued, "Turner Pond is just a few miles up the road. I take my pram over to the mainland and drive my truck to the spring. It ain't such a much. In the summer, ya know, I only lug drinking water. I take my baths in the pond even if it's cold. It don't bother me none. Hell, they ain't nothin' on me that gets hard anymore anyway."

We went back to his cabin, where he finally began to talk about his wife. "We're plenty close," Aime smiled. "She just doesn't want to stay out here. She comes in and cleans the cabin about once a year, I don't know what for. I keep it as clean as I want. Besides, the roof leaks by the chimney, and it just gets dirty again. Last time she was in, ya know, I told her if she lost any more weight, I was going to have to marry another woman. She only tips the scales at eighty-five pounds."

I laughed to myself listening to Aime joke about Angelina, recognizing that his kind of kidding comes only from couples who have made a good life together. I wondered if Angelina talked as much as he did. It would be interesting to hear her chew his ear off for not keeping the cabin cleaner. And it would be just as interesting to observe Aime's facial expressions as he sat there listening.

It was now six o'clock. Aime and I had been talking since noon. I had been trying to break away for an hour. I wanted to get off the pond and dirt roads before dark.

"Listen," I told him, rising from the table, "I have got to get going. That pond is still rough, and I need to get off it before dark."

"Right you are. Once you get my talkin' machine a-goin', I can't stop it." Aime followed me out the door.

"If you try to cut diagonally across the pond, you'll miss your take-out," Aime said. He untied the bow of my canoe and pushed me off, talking right to the end. "The wind will blow you right by it. Paddle straight to the mainland, then follow the shoreline around to your truck."

It had been a long day.

Sitting in the canoe and leaning into my paddle, I chewed on a peanut-butter sandwich. Across the state from this mountain pond, the early morning sun first touches America. During the late afternoon, red shimmering rays from sunsets filter through the trees and cast long shadows on its waters. As I drifted away from shore and began to paddle, I thought how the island's solitude reminded me of the loneliness of being away from home during the hellish year I spent in Vietnam.

Looking back at Aime, walking back toward his cabin, head bowed, I thought of his loneliness and his parting words:

"Come back sometime when ya can set and jaw a spell. I don't get much company up this way."

Aime's words brought a moist film to my eyes. They reminded me of Dad's parting words as I left home on my way to Vietnam. He said, "Son, if I could I'd go in your place." Then he turned, head bowed, and walked to the car. It was time for me to go.

Aime died on the island in 1993, before I got back to visit him. He was almost 92.

Charlie Reitze

(Beach at Englishman Bay)

Chapter Two
Dawn At Roque Bluffs
Living Our Dream

In Englishman Bay off the coast of Washington County, a sailboat at anchor bobbed like a buoy in rough seas while the silver rays of the sun left wispy trails of vapor over her deck. Whitecaps roared up on the sandy beach, puddling around a middle-aged lady's feet as she took a morning stroll.

Unlike my flashbacks on the road to Holeb Pond, here I felt peaceful, comfortable. I seemed to be in my element. It wasn't unlike my recuperation after the Tet Offensive at Cam Ranh Bay on the South China Sea. The sandy shores. The sea breeze. The Tranquility. I experienced inner visions of running barefoot on the sandy beaches of Watchic Lake during my childhood and roaming peacefully through the mountains and lakes of Western Maine during my teenage years. I sat for a while meditating, soaking in the warmth.

By nine o'clock, I was walking with a lady on the beach, soaking my feet in the salt water. Looking up, she said, "See how the clouds, scattered around pockets of blue, look like a knitted quilt."

By ten, I flagged down a mailman, who was snaking his way around the bay, stuffing envelopes in dented mailboxes.

"She's a hummer of a day, ain't she?" said the mailman.

"I reckon she is," I answered, my feet still bare. "If I had the time, I'd lie on the beach all day, but I'm trying to find the Hunts. You wouldn't happen to know where they live? Some people at the health-food store in Machias told me that they live out this way."

"They do, but you're going to need a canoe."

"Isn't there some kind of a trail?"

"Yeah! There's some kind of a trail, all right." The mailman said. "It's an old muddy road and footpath that follows the river up from the bay. But you better have hip boots or you're gonna get awful wet."

The ledges where the mailman told me to park my truck were about a quarter-mile down an old dirt road. Dressed in white corduroys and a white T-Shirt, my Canon camera slung over my shoulder, I crossed the ledges, rounded a bend, and stared at a trail of mud and moose tracks, hedged in by thick, overhanging conifers. After seeing how muddy the trail was, I returned to Festus, stripped off my corduroys, put on my cutoffs, and struck out again. The mud was ankle-deep in most places, and even deeper where the suction pulled off my sneaker. Three times the trail left the woods, coming out into an estuary, and three times I got on my hands and knees, sighting through the muddy swale grass, trying to relocate the trail.

The thick undergrowth, the heavy forest, the mud, and swale, all brought back haunting memories of Vietnam. But here there was a delightful ambiance; here I carried a camera, not a rifle; here I wore cut-offs, not full-length camo; here I wore sneakers, not high, green boots; here I wore a green, L.L. Bean Stetson, not a neck-breaking hard hat; and here, even though it was muddy, the bushes, thick, and the mosquitoes, rampant — everything in place to trigger nightmares — I didn't have any. I was happy. I was enjoying myself. I was still reveling in my morning walk.

(Footpath and Railing to Hunt's Place)

I walked over three, twelve-inch-wide footbridges as I crossed creeks that meandered to the sea and listened to the gurgling water. I came into one final swale area, peaked through fir trees and saw a wood-shingled house on the opposite side.

I was disappointed to find no one home. The door wasn't locked and I was hungry and thirsty, so I timidly let myself in, ate a banana, and drank a couple glasses of water. I found a map on the table which showed a shorter, drier way to the house. I left a note on the map explaining who I was, and a dollar on the counter for the food.

By four o'clock, no one had shown up. The late afternoon sky had developed a pink hue. My camera was empty and the tide was coming in. It was time to go. I stuffed my T-shirt into my camera bag. The sea breeze felt clean and refreshing against my skin. As I walked along, I felt like a mountainous weight had been lifted from off of my shoulders. No longer were bullets whizzing by like so many angry hornets. No longer were tracer rounds lighting up the night sky. No longer did screams of terror fill the air. No longer was I on corrupted soil. Here, I was free to appreciate the peace of nature – here, I was... free.

By six o'clock, I was enjoying a hot shower and singing, "In the mud and the blood and the beer" by Johnny Cash at the Seagull Motel in Machias.

The next morning, I tried again and found the Hunts at home.

(Butch and Rachelle Hunt's place)

Rachelle greeted me at the door.

"Hi," I said, anxiously. "Sorry to be here so early, but I didn't want you to leave before I had a chance to see you. I'm the guy who ate your banana yesterday."

"Oh, that's okay," said Rachelle, a slender woman, with a

plump face and long, light brown hair. She wore a loose-fitting blouse with blue jeans. "Come on in. We took bets on how early you'd be here. Butch is getting dressed. He said you would be here early. I wasn't so sure."

Coming from the bedroom, Butch scratched his head and yawned. "I was sitting down meditating," he said. "I do that every morning."

Butch wore farmer trousers, held up with red suspenders and a checkered flannel shirt. He was sinew-thin and a little taller than Rachelle. His hair and full beard were both scraggly and coal black. And his smile and laugh were as exuberant as Rachelle's.

Neither Butch nor Rachelle were native Mainers. The couple moved here to escape the changing Massachusetts in the sixties.

Butch grew up south of Boston in Marshfield. Rachelle grew up in Allston, also a suburb of Boston. They met in college.

"Neither of us liked it in Marshfield," Butch said, sliding bowls onto the table and sitting down for breakfast. "I remember my fourth-grade teacher asking us what we wanted to be when we grew up. It was all very conventional until she got to me. I said, 'I'm gonna live way out in the woods and be a trapper.' At adolescence, I wanted a girl who would live in the woods, but didn't think I'd find one."

"But you did!" Rachelle said, and smiled at Butch with an "Oh baby, I love to love you" twinkle in her eyes.

"We both wanted to move out of the city," she said. "It was during the Vietnam War era. There were riots in the streets, a big recession, and I was developing health problems. With all the mess going on, I dreaded getting up mornings and couldn't wait for weekends. As a child, I used to walk north ten to fifteen miles every Saturday. I got so far away that Dad had to come pick me up. People are too separated from the earth by society's hustle and bustle, their fax machines and telephones. You don't see anything like that around here," said Rachelle, sweeping her arm in a wide arc. "We find those things jarring, and the bill enslavement that goes with them. We never felt like we belonged. Now we do. We're home."

And for the first time since Vietnam, so was I. Even though I knew there was still a lot of healing yet ahead, I had begun to find a peace with these people who lived in the woods. These were a people who made me feel like I belonged. They loved me for who I was, and didn't hate me for where I had been. I suppose I must have been off in my own little world for a few minutes when Rachelle broke the silence.

"You must have had quite a trip in here yesterday," Rachelle said, pouring hot cereal in our bowls. "I'm sorry we weren't here. We went canoeing with some friends. You picked the only day of the year that one of us wasn't here."

"It was quite a day. I did get a bit muddy," I said. "The trail I took yesterday was wet. I thought about taking a bath in the river but I was worried you might come home.

"We swim in the river. When we first moved here, the locals had it going around that we were having orgies. Our friends came up from Massachusetts to help us build. There were seven of us, and four dogs. We all took baths in the stream together and used the sweat lodge that you saw down by the guest house. Some of the locals were nosy and came up to see what was going on. They saw us through binoculars and thought we were rich eccentrics."

"Do you consider yourselves eccentrics?"

"No," Rachelle said. "We moved in during the hippie movement, but we were not part of that." We're not hermits or eccentrics. We're just living our dream. The locals know that now. It took a few years, but we're accepted. Hey, it was four local couples who built our new footbridge that you walked over this morning."

Butch and Rachelle's happiness bubbled like a boiling teakettle. They were smiling, grinning, laughing, and loved talking about their lives, not because they were lonesome and needed someone to talk to, but because they are able to do what they always dreamed of doing.

"Rachelle went to school in Boston for a while, and then transferred to Paier Art School in Connecticut, where I went to school," he said. "After graduating, we worked at Rust Craft Greeting Cards for almost a year as cartoonists. That's where we met. We both got fired, and that's when we moved up here."

That was 1973. A close friend from Massachusetts had bought the land they now own while he attended school in Machias. The Hunts later bought it from him. With help from friends, they built a raft, floated building supplies a mile up the Englishman River at high tide and built the house on three and two-thirds acres of land for less than eight thousand dollars.

Their house sits on the edge of a grassy peninsula with a thick-forested background of conifers, a little over a mile from the coast. From the living room and kitchen, there is a 270-degree view of the estuary, and they can watch deer, moose, bear, ducks, and geese along the banks of the Englishman River that switchbacks through the tall swale grasses on its way to the ocean. Moving up the knoll to their house, the swale grass is crowded out by the greener timothy hedging in their small garden. A long, narrow wooden table loaded with rocks for Rachelle's paintings sits in front of an empty woodshed just outside the front door.

(Roque Bluffs Estuary)

From the kitchen table, I could see the estuary, the front yard, and the interior layout of the house in a single glance. The outside walls were open studding with no insulation. Everything was tongue-and-groove boards with mortise-and-tenon joints and oak pegs holding the posts and beams together.

"It's mostly the old post-and-beam-construction-type home," Rachelle said, as she got up from the table and headed to the sink with our bowls. "We wanted it done old-fashioned. We didn't know what we were doing, but one of the guys who helped us was a carpenter. He planned things out, like building the living room and kitchen L-shaped around the bedroom and mudroom for better air circulation.

That's why the chimney and woodstove are in the middle of the house." Rachelle pointed toward their Palmina woodstove. "That stove is so big and the heat circulates so well that we don't need insulation. It's great for cooking, too."

Butch added, "We cut the dying trees during the year and bring in a couple cords of hardwood slabs by canoe before winter sets in."

A gas cooking stove sat opposite the oversized cast-iron kitchen sink, while a gas refrigerator sat in front of the entryway. There were two gas lights--one over the kitchen area and one over the dining area. This was all Butch and Rachelle needed for comfort. Their only source of water was a hand pump beside the sink. The water came from a well about twenty feet behind the house.

"Come on out back," Butch said. "We'll show you the well. I had a vision. An image came to me just before going to bed one night. I saw where the well should be and about how deep to dig. We dug about nine feet, which is about how deep I saw, and hit more water than we could bail out."

I followed Butch and Rachelle out behind the house, going down over a small embankment and around a few stumps to the well. "It's rocked up with flat rocks from out in the bay," Rachelle said, pointing to the neatly placed rocks that lined the well. "We hauled them in on our canoes, like we do everything else."

"We have a two-canoe system," Butch said. We turned and walked past the house, the garden, and down a footpath to where the two canoes were stashed beside the stream.

Pointing to the upside-down canoes, Butch said, "We hook them up like a catamaran, like a float. With both canoes hooked together, they'll float a ton. We haul everything that way — our food, stoves, wood, rocks, everything. When high tide comes, we go downstream, get whatever, and pole back up. All the heavy stuff, we haul in the summer. In the winter, it's not so easy to haul things in. We bring stuff in on a toboggan the way you came in yesterday. It's a mile-and-a-half walk. We have people who can't find this place on that trail. Once you get into the marsh, you can't see where to walk."

"Boy, do I know that feeling!" I said. "Yesterday I had to get down on my knees to locate the trail where the high tide had washed out almost any trace of it."

"We'd come in the way you did today," Rachelle added, "if they plowed the snow off the Duck Cove Road where our trail comes out of the woods. It's a two-and-a-half-mile drive that way, but only a third-of-a-mile walk."

"We haul in cow manure, too," Rachelle said, pointing back at the garden. "We use it to supplement the seaweed that Butch gets. He takes a canoe out before high tide and sets old trees in the stream for booms to catch seaweed. It makes wonderful fertilizer. He gets about fifty bushels a summer. Between it and the cow manure, we have a good garden. We grow most of our vegetables."

It took eight years for the Hunts to "get all the kinks out" and learn how to survive well in the woods. At first they did not know how to grow vegetables, live without electricity, or cook with wood.

"We were as green as grass," Rachelle said, while walking back to the house. "We learned the hard way, by experience and failure. The first five years, I thought we had made a terrible mistake. We felt trapped because we had spent all our money on this place, and there was no way out. We had no right-of-way and no road, so no one would buy it. Now, people approach us and want to buy it, but now we don't want to sell."

Rachelle handed me a brochure they wrote for their art business. It read:

From our window we watch bobcat, deer, moose, eagles, lynx, coyote, otter — about every creature indigenous to Maine — and the birding is fantastic.

Our dream was to become wildlife artists and to be able to sustain a living while working in our home. This has been realized by giving up most of the modern luxuries — electricity, running water, phone, even a drivable road to the house. Doing it this way bought us time by cutting costs, allowing us to practice our art.

We started living simply to save money. Now, after all these years, we have found much more. We would not trade all the luxuries of the world for the beauty, quiet, and power of Nature as it surrounds and penetrates us with its being.

Rachelle (Bourque) and Bernard (Butch) Hunt's brochure seems a fitting description of many people who live in the woods of Maine. They are all living their own dream.

Last year Butch and Rachelle earned nine thousand dollars from their wildlife paintings. They paint on canvas and on special rhyolite rocks that are peculiar to the area. They sell their paintings at the Woodland Gallery in Machias and at art shows throughout the state. Butch digs a few clams to supplement their painting income and Rachelle cooks for Sunrise Canoe Expeditions. They both agree that they would be comfortable on twelve thousand dollars. But Butch said, "We could probably be healthier on less than that. But we like to drink wine and brandy, and I make our own beer."

As I listened to Butch and Rachelle — knowing that they

had moved to Roque Bluffs only a few years after I returned home from Vietnam — I thought yet again of an old trapper who told me to "do whatever it is you want to do."

Looking out their window at swale grass bending in the ocean breeze, I realized the rice paddies of Vietnam were really gone. They lay somewhere behind a "veil of tears," where I would only return if I carelessly let myself drift into the past.

As I stepped out the door to leave, Rachelle said, "It's probably your love of the outdoors, your desire to be free — to share this type of life with others — that brought you here. I think it's that same love that will take you to wherever you go next."

I've lost track of the Hunts over the years. I hope they're still healthy and living their dreams.

Chapter Three
Mountain Pond
Interlude

After leaving the Hunts, I wanted to be alone for a while. So I drove to Greenville and hired Folsoms' Air Service to fly me into a small, secluded pond, Mountain Pond. There, on a mossy knoll, I built a lean-to out of spruce boughs, bundled my clothes up in a plastic Shop 'N Save grocery bag, threw them in the lean-to, dove in the pond, and went skinny dipping for most of the day.

In a pensive mood, I left the outside world behind and spent the next seven days on R&R (a military term for rest and recuperation) – swimming in the cool, fresh waters of Mountain Pond, trying to figure out how I could climb up the back of a big bull moose as he swam toward shore, hiking the surrounding hills, thinking, eating fresh trout, meditating, eating blueberries, raspberries, reading, and writing — writing the spiritual thoughts that came as I laid on my back and soaked up the sun.

At my campsite, I read William Least Heat-Moon's book, *PrairyErth*. One part read:

> *"Once in his life a man ought to concentrate his mind upon the remembered earth, I believe. He ought to give himself up to a particular landscape in his experience, to look at it from as many angles as he can, to wonder about it, to dwell upon it. He ought to imagine that he touches it with his hands at every season and listens to*

*the sounds that are made upon it. He ought to imagine
the creatures there and all the faintest motions of the
wind. He ought to recollect the glare of noon and all the
colors of the dawn and dusk."*

When I began writing, a double portrait emerged: one of
my youth, Vietnam, the people who represented the
sacredness of my beliefs, and one of the lake, the stream, the
sunset and sunrise, the flora and fauna and of Maine's great
North Woods, the woods that since my childhood, have held
me within its embrace.

Lying on my back on a mossy knoll on which I had built
my lean-to, I watched the marshmallow-fluffy clouds collide,
mesh, and float along, carefree in a sky of paradise blue.
While writing, I tried to become one with my surroundings. I
met nature on her terms, sometimes clothed, sometimes not,
but always clothed with naturalness, like all of Mother
Earth. I tried to understand her deepest intimacies, her
secrets, her dreams, her softest whispers. I gave myself up to
the moment, to the enfolding landscape, to the pine-scented
mountain air, until I meshed with my surroundings. I
searched for words to convey the beauty, the oneness of the
life that has always held me in awe.

It was here in my meditations that I began to understand
my own mortality. We're not stone faces on Mt. Rushmore.
We're people who have our agency. Sometimes we're
inclined to live in the past because the path to the future can
be so difficult.

Or, we can choose to chart another course. I found it was
futile to relive the old, and quite dangerous to try to
obliterate it. I found that I had the capacity to make things
anew. My spiritual survival required me to turn away from

the dooming mind-repetitions of the past.

Mountain Pond was now. It was the beginning of the future. It was here that I charted my course. I somehow knew, "The place to begin was where life treated me the best."

I needed to return to church.

(Moose.)

Charlie Reitze

(Sunset at Mountain Pond.)

Chapter Four
Solon
Creep City

I found Creep City much like everyplace else — by hunting for the next place that would fit the parameters of my book, that is, there could be no electricity outside of their own making (which included a generator) and there could be no roads. Where the roads are concerned, I made an exception for Creep City, partly because the name intrigued me, partly because of what I had been told about it, and partly because it was a bit of a hamlet of its own and off the beaten path of what society considers the norm.

I was visiting Nowetah's Indian Store in New Portland, which is a small town in Somerset County, where I met Donald Black, a Penobscot Indian. He was building a birch-bark tepee.

"If you're hunting for backwoods folks," Don said, "check out Creep City in Solon. It's a whole community of back-to-the-landers."

"Solon," I repeated, scratching my head. "I used to live there. I've never heard of Creep City."

Don turned and peered at me through dark shades under his cowboy hat. "The only reason I know about it is because I drive a school bus, and one of the kids told me. I've never been there either."

"Do you have any idea how it got the name, Creep City?"

"I'm not sure," Don replied, "but I heard it was

something about a kid calling some guy who lived there a creep."

As we walked toward Festus, Don pointed to the *Maine Atlas* I was holding open. "That's where they are. When you come to a big mailbox with 4040 on it, turn right. It will take you into Creep City."

"I really don't know much about the place," Don said. "I hear most of the folks teach school. There's supposed to be one real nice house back there. They don't have any electricity and I've heard they have a community bathhouse. That's about all I know."

After leaving Don I had all kinds of crazy thoughts about this place called Creep City. I remember thinking, a community bath house. What am I getting myself into? Do they let you go after you get there? And I wasn't about to get into a community bath house. I decided I'd go no matter what. So I headed to Solon.

Solon is a small town of about a 1,000 to 1,500 people north of Skowhegan on Route 201. It was maybe 20 miles from New Portland.

After going through Solon when the winding blacktop stopped, the Brighton Road turned into hard-packed snow over dirt and continued to snake northeast through small hills toward Brighton Plantation. After four or five miles, I stopped at an old tin-roofed, tarpaper-sided cabin to ask directions.

A tall, stern-looking man wearing a hunter's stocking cap, faded jeans, and an unbuttoned flannel shirt emerged from the cabin. He walked leaning on a crooked, apple wood cane that he grasped with his right hand. Before I said anything, he came over to me, stuck his face so close to mine that our noses almost touched, and asked curtly, "Who are you? You ain't one of them witfits, are ya?'"

(Bruce Morris lives in the suburbs of Creep City.)

"What's a 'witfit'?" I asked, matching his stare and tone.

"A Jehovah Witness!"

"No, I'm not a witfit," I said laughing. I'm looking for Creep City."

"Well, that makes a difference. I'll talk to you then," he said, backing off to a more comfortable distance and easing his harsh tone.

"I'm just working on a story," I said. "Is this part of Creep City?"

"Nope. I call this the suburbs."

"Is this the only place in the suburbs?" I asked, grinning.

"Yup," he said. "I never liked a crowd. Come on in and set a spell. We don't have to stand out here in the cold shootin' the shit."

I agreed. Stepping into his cabin, I noticed a sign on the door. Painted in two-inch block letters, it read:

GONE TO TOWN
NO JEHOVER WITFITS ALLOWED!

He wiped his hand on his trousers and then extended it to shake mine. "I'm Bruce Morris. I live here with Noreen Atwood. She's working at the boarding home in Solon."

"Have a seat," he said and then settled into his own chair. "We've been here for years. I came here to give up drinking. I drank for twenty years after Vietnam, and that was too long. Vietnam was a strange place to be. The hardest thing I had to do when I came home was give up drinking. I don't talk about 'Nam much," Bruce said, pouring a cup of coffee for himself, hot chocolate for me, and abruptly changing the subject. "I like it here. We've got no power and no phone."

"I used to go to town quite often when I was drinking," Bruce said. "Only time I go to town now is if I need somethin'. We don't need much. We have a big garden, and I cut the winter's wood from right around here, so most of the time I stay home. I'm building Noreen a bedroom now." Bruce pointed to a pile of lumber in the living room. "See, I'm building it off that wall there, so we won't have to sleep in the living room anymore."

Bruce was fairly tall and lanky. He was tough. Buried not far beneath his gruffness was a gentle, kind, well of emotions ready to spill over. When he mentioned Vietnam, he got teary-eyed. When I mentioned Vietnam, I got teary-eyed. We couldn't discuss it much. Neither of us wanted to.

•••••

Bruce was like "Pop" — one of my closest friends in Vietnam. Every time Bruce smiled, I saw Pop. We gave Pop his nickname because he was in his mid-twenties while the rest of us in 'Nam were around nineteen.

Pop was a sweet guy. He was one of those guys that you'd take a bullet for. The day after the Tet Offensive, Pop, in a soft voice, asked me, tears streaming down his cheeks, "Why? Charlie, why? Three good men are dead. And look at Escamilla, he's no more than a vegetable. Why? Why do these things have to happen?" Pop's thin frame trembled as he spoke. "And Charlie," he said, aghast, "The people back home don't understand. They hate us. Look at what's going on back there. They call us baby killers. We didn't ask to be here."

"I don't have any answers, Pop," I said, as I wiped tears from my eyes. "I just don't know."

And I didn't know. I'm not certain that I know now. I

don't know that anyone really does. But I do know that I was serving my country, and I'm proud of that. And I also know that Vietnam isn't going to ruin me now. At Baker Pond, I paddled my way from the past into the future. At Mountain Pond, I set my course. I decided to go back to church.

Pop and I shed many tears. We still do. We probably always will. We shed tears – tears of great reverence for the men who died in Vietnam, tears of great respect for those who came home never to be completely whole again, and bitter tears knowing that even our closest friends and family members will never really understand.

Sitting side-by-side, Pop and I flew home on the same flight. We flew out of Bien Hoa. I said to Pop, "I won't feel comfortable until we're above shooting range." He just smiled. A few hours later we landed in Okinawa, Japan. The first thing I did was order two banana splits. Pop went to the rest room. He was so long in there that I had eaten half of my split when I went to see what was keeping him. "Pop, what are you doing?"

"I'm flushing the toilet, Charlie. I ain't seen one of these for a year. I been flushing it and flushing it and flushing it."

Pop stepped out of the stall, half-grinning, half-crying. He looked at me, and we both broke down. Each of us knew what the other was thinking. In our minds rockets exploded and tracer rounds lit the sky. In our sleep, screams woke us, and death stared us in the face. Even though the physical fighting was over, the memories weren't. And it scared us. We both sensed that the biggest battles lay ahead, the battles within ourselves. In Vietnam, quite often, long periods of silence, aloofness, was all that passed between us. Sometimes we just wanted to be alone. I still do. Even today, I often feel the need to escape to our family camp in the woods.

Pop and I never finished our splits. We had to get back on that old, uncomfortable, Air Force cargo jet. There were four rows of seats on those planes. Each row stretched the full length of the plane. Two rows of men sat with their backs to the outside walls. Two rows sat with their backs to the center. We were jammed in elbow to elbow. It was anything but comfortable. But, hey, we were going home. At our next stop, Anchorage, Alaska, we were finally back in the states. We were almost home.

Now, twenty-plus years later, I sat talking to Bruce, another veteran who, like me, lived off the grid. He too, needed his space. He needed to be where he could cry, if he wanted. And like all the rest of us, he needed someone who could understand, and that someone was Noreen.

"You said this was the suburbs of Creep City. Where exactly is Creep City? And what are the people like who live there?"

"Oh you hear all kinds of stories but they're all really nice people."

•••••

"Anyway, it's just up the road a piece. When you come to the mailbox with 4040 on it, you turn right. That's the Creep City superhighway — dirt, one-lane, and a dead-end. You can't get lost, and you won't have any trouble gettin' down in there. They plow their own road, cut their own wood, and take their own kids to school. They do everything together."

(Creep City Snow Plow.)

"Here, take this apple-wood cane." Bruce abruptly changed the subject. "It's slippery out and you might need it."

The cane had a corkscrew shape, with an S-curve to it. The grip was about five inches from where the cane was bent at a ninety-degree angle. Looking at Bruce, I smiled, knowing I had made a friend.

When I got back in my truck, Bruce shut the door for me. "If you see any of them witfits, you tell 'em I ain't home."

•••••

It was only a quarter-mile from Bruce's to the mailbox numbered 4040. The Creep City road wasn't unlike a beautiful farm driveway: two-wheel ruts, a grassy hump in the middle, and neat rows of towering maples along white fences. Creep City's entrance was straight and narrow like a farm's, but instead of wheel ruts and a grass hump, it was sheet ice, not sanded, and tunneled between five-foot snow banks and scattered trees. Sled-runner tracks revealed its present use.

Steering the right front tire into the snow bank on the edge of the road to gain some control, I crept down the long, gradual hill. Halfway down, a woman with a "stop or I'll shoot" expression stood knee-deep in the snow, hands planted on her hips and elbows stuck out like Annie Oakley ready to quick-draw. I wasn't sure if I wanted to stop, but I did, after sliding about twenty feet.

"How much farther is Creep City?" I asked quickly, but in a pleasant tone.

"Who are you?" she replied. "Are you from Hawaii?"

Hawaii? Why would she ask me that?

"No, I'm not from Hawaii," I said. "I'm working on a book."

"Well, I'm not interested, but some of the others might be. We're expecting someone from Hawaii. I'm Linda Helmir. Goodbye."

She started back up the hill again, but turned and shouted, "Don't run over the kids! They're all sliding in the middle of the road down around the corner. There's a bunch of them."

"Off to my left I saw one house, to my right behind a pond was another. The smoke filtering through the treetops provided evidence that other houses were hidden in a forest of conifers surrounding the small community.

(Kids of Creep City Sliding in the Middle of the Road.)

I considered turning back until I rounded the bend at the bottom of the hill and saw the kids Linda warned me about. A dozen of them, screaming and happy, were sliding in the middle of the road. They used sleds, mixing bowls, and their South ends. Not daring to drive past them, I parked Festus and walked around and between them, hoping they wouldn't run over me. One kid started sliding down the hill when I had almost reached the bottom. Another yelled, "Don't run over that flatlander, you might splatter him all over our road and mess up the slidin'."

Grinning, I jumped into a snow bank just as a grinning tyke sped past me with malicious intent written all over his face. The other kids followed in quick succession, screaming.

One yelled to another, "Hey, wipe your nose; it's running faster than you can eat of it."

Walking up the far side of the hill, I saw two more houses. A man walking toward me introduced himself – rather pleasantly, I thought, compared to Linda's greeting – as Richard Roberts. I remained apprehensive, but unlike Linda, Richard's voice was welcoming. He was thin and stood over six feet tall. He had dark brown hair, and seemed as talkative as Johnny Carson. A few minutes later, a woman walked over, curious to see the visitor. Richard introduced me to Elley Howell.

"Oh, good," Elley said with a stoic expression, as she stood there, a foot shorter than Richard. "Another one! We've had folks like you here before. We never tell them the truth, and they never get to leave!"

I didn't say anything. I didn't quite believe her, but she was putting on a good act. For a few seconds there was an awkward silence – eerie and uncomfortable, for me at least.

I guess Elley sensed it, or my facial expression gave me away because she broke out in laughter and ended the silence. "Oh, no! I'm just kidding. You're more than welcome. Then she just out-of-nowhere launched into a whole new subject: "That cemetery was part of the old farm. Here, let me take you through it."

Oh boy, I thought, *I wonder if they've already got a hole dug for people like me.* I wanted to tell her that I would live just as long and die just as happy if we didn't, but she had already grabbed my hand and pulled me along. Looking at the tilting headstones in the front part of the cemetery, I read one inscription, "Fanny, wife of David Gilman, died on April 14, 1887, 89 years, 9 months old. Rest Tired Mother." I knew I wasn't that tired and was glad when we left. I think

Elley was just having fun running me through the cemetery first.

(Creep City Cemetery)

We walked back to where Richard was helping a boy fix his flatlander-attack sled. Elley left, but told me to come visit her after I finished with Richard and Martha."

Martha Maloney, Richard's fiancée, was in her mid-thirties. She's just a shade shorter than Richard, just as thin, and has the same dark wavy hair. She met us at the door and gave me a quick tour of their home. It looked like a ski-slope hideaway — quaint, with curved living-room walls. The outside wall was a bank of disassembled sliding glass door windows, affording a halcyon view of the western mountains. Two twelve-volt battery systems, charged by a solar panel, ran the TV set.

(Martha Maloney and Richard Roberts)

As I sat down at the kitchen table, Martha offered me a glass of cold water while Richard continued to talk. "We're both from Ohio. We met at Kent State, where I was working on my English degree. Martha earned her degree there in art and music. I'm finishing mine at the University of Maine at Farmington."

"We were originally moving to Quebec City," Martha said, sitting down with the water, "so I could learn French. But on the way, and luckily not too far from here, we had a small accident with the car. We wired the car together and came here because Richard had a friend who was a mechanic. We stayed because we liked it. The people here were fun to be around. They helped us and we helped them."

Pointing out the living-room window toward the distant mountains, Richard added, "And that's not the only reason. Look at the view out there. If our friends aren't enough to make us stay, that view is all the reason we need. It's the same for everyone else — it's pleasant here, it's peaceful, there are no trucks going by, the kids don't get in trouble, we don't breathe smog all day, and we don't have big bills. But we do have all we want or need. What more could anyone ask?"

"We even have a phone," Martha said, thumbing through the phone book. "I wanted it in case of emergencies, so Richard hooked it up. It's not just for us. Everyone in the village uses it."

"It works off an antenna on the roof. The antenna is pointed at a base tower three miles away," Richard explained, sliding the phone across the table to me. "See, it's like a cordless phone, only it doesn't broadcast in a circle. There used to be a lot of static on the phone, but when I put the thermax insulation under the house, it somehow created better reception. Now we can hear good. There's hardly any static at all."

"What kind of electrical system do you have?" I asked,

looking at the TV in the living room.

"The wiring in each house is set up with a battery electric system," Richard answered. "We only use it for the boob tube. We run everything else on gas. There's not much to see, just a bunch of batteries hooked together. We charge them in Solon at the local garage. But let me show you how we built the house."

Following Richard, we went from the kitchen, through the living room, into the bathroom. Richard picked up an old chain saw in a closet next to the tub. "Martha and I built the old part of the house with this. She did most of the chain saw work. We're building the new part when we're not working at our outside jobs."

"I work as an alternate education teacher with dropouts at the local school," Richard said. "I like a challenge, and it's more of a challenge than a regular classroom."

"While he's teaching," Martha said, "I weave and sell baskets. We like our jobs, and we like it here. In the winter, we all get together and slide in bowls with the kids. In the summer, we swim in the mud pond. Everyone has a great time. And we get to work on the house whenever we want."

Time with Martha and Richard was short because they needed to drive to Skowhegan to buy some basket material.

I took Elley up on her invitation and wandered over to her house. She stood in her yard alongside a handsome young man who rested his chin on her shoulder. The boy was her teenage son, Ethan. Their dog watched me with his brown head cocked sideways between Ethan's knees, reminiscent of a scene from "Lassie, Come Home."

Elley, a short woman of maybe five-foot two or three inches tall had plump red cheeks, and medium-brown hair pulled back in a bow. She seemed to wear a constant smile.

Elley grew up in North Anson, but moved to Creep City with a man she met from the area. She was in her early forties. Ethan stood head and shoulders taller than his mom.

(Elley and son, Ethan, Howell and First Dog Marieka.)

"This is First Dog Marieka." Elley said, reaching over and patting the dog, that now stood on hind legs with big front paws planted on Ethan's chest. "He's kind of spoiled."

"Come on in," she said. "Let's have some hot chocolate. You must be cold. We watched from the kitchen window while you jump started Richard's car. Martha told me they needed to go to town, but she wasn't sure how they were going to get their car started. It was forty-below last night."

"Those snotty-nosed curtain-climbers almost ran over you with their sleds and bowls, didn't they?" Elley asked, rhetorically.

"Yeah they were having fun," I said.

She sat down next to Ethan, poured three mugs of hot

chocolate and then jumped back up to let the dog out.

"It's a great life here," Elley said. "And the kids have their fun without getting into trouble. That's one of the reasons we like it. We're down on booze, drugs, and cigarettes, and high on days to come. Sometimes the kids say, 'Oh my God! We can't wait to get outta here. We're going somewhere where there's running water.' Then she added, "We're going to get them all back. The kids realize what they have, and they all return."

"That's right," said Athena Etingen-Van Den Bossche, almost as if on cue. She had overheard our conversation while lugging in firewood.

Athena, 22 is of Russian and Belgian descent. She was actually born in Athens, but moved to Creep City when she was three. She initially lived in a tepee while her parents finished building their house.

"The Van Den Bossche in my name is Flemish and means 'of the woods.' I don't know what the first part of my name means, but it's Russian."

She left Creep City to attend Antioch College, but returned after graduating in 1992. Her parents, had divorced and moved away, but she lives in their old home.

"I came back," she said, "partly because of the practical knowledge I gained here that you don't get in college. Here I learned how to deliver babies, play music and plant a garden. I can live off the land. And the community is like a tribe. Everything is a communal effort. We take care of our elders and each other. The other kids who have grown up here don't feel much different," Athena said, as she headed toward the door. "They say they want a home here, too, even if it's just a base to come back to. We're all a big family."

She was gone as quickly as she had come.

Shaking the grates on the woodstove, Elley said, "Sometimes Athena brings me kindling wood. She'll be by and visit a little later. She's a good kid. I feel bad for city kids and folks who will never know what these kids have."

"All most people see up here," Ethan spoke for the first time, "is the end of the world, but to us it's just the beginning. We've got a totally different way of doing things. It's hard at times, but I like it. I've learned things that other kids at my school don't have a clue about. I can take care of animals, cut wood, work on the house — a lot of stuff."

"And it's easier raising the kids," Elley added, smiling at Ethan. "We don't have the trouble here that they do with kids growing up in bigger towns. Our kids aren't off racing cars, doing drugs, stealing, or sitting in front of a computer playing games all day. They grow up learning the value of work. I'm not saying they're perfect or better than anyone else, or that they don't complain some like kids do. But I am saying that their work habits have bred good study habits and, between both, they keep out of trouble and get better grades than most other kids their age. We live here because we want to, not because we have to."

Elley called her home the "Tarpaper Mansion." She's been working on an addition for five years. "When it's completed," she said, leaning back in her chair and sipping hot chocolate, "I'll begin remodeling the old part, installing insulated windows and doors. This year I'm building a new woodshed and private bathhouse combination, with a gas hot-water heater and generator."

"I do it as I can," Elley said, picking up a receipt from the table. "I'm not putting myself into debt, but I wouldn't mind a few creature comforts. Now there are no inside toilets. We all have outhouses. Really, I don't mind. I sit out there with my coffee, watching the deer eat off the apple trees. It wakes me up. We haul all our firewood with ponies, lug our water, and plow our own road. I wouldn't trade it for anything."

"You don't have a community bathhouse then?" I asked, grinning sheepishly, not knowing how she would take the question.

"Not hardly," Ethan said, setting his mug down hard with a big smile. "It doesn't surprise me that you heard something like that. But it ain't true. We either take sponge baths or lug water for our own tubs. People don't have any idea what it's like here, so they dream up all kinds of stupid things. Most of the things they say are kind of funny. We call them the 'Ignorant Funnies.'"

"Where do you work?" I asked, taking some cookies from the jar Elley slid down to me from the head of the table.

"At the Last Unicorn Restaurant in Waterville, and the Solon Hotel, as a bartender. That gives me all I need. Last summer I had a 'burn-the-mortgage' party. The whole community came. We had a huge bonfire, a potluck supper, and everyone hooted and hollered when I burned my mortgage."

Elley was also a percussionist and vocalist in a five-woman *a cappella* comedy group called the "Twatones." They played all over New England and had a mini Mardi Gras at Athens, Maine, every summer. Lee Sharkey, one of my English professors at the University of Maine at Farmington knew the people at Creep City. She once told me, "I first heard them play at the Athens Fourth of July fair. They were bawdy and funny, harmonic and dissident, a musical show with day-glo sunglasses. Their costumes were a mockery of femininity. They sang concocted conventional songs with affection and merciless parody."

Elley was talking about the Mardi Gras when the front door suddenly burst open. A girl ran in, screaming, "You can tell the city kids are here, one of them got hurt! She's laying flat out." She motioned with her hands like an umpire calling safe. "She's dead! I know she's dead!"

Just then the hurt child ran through the door, holding her hands over her face and bawling.

"Got any broken bones?" Elley asked, going to comfort the little girl.

"No," she cried, tears running down her face. "Just a frozen face smack. I drove my face right into the snow."

"Oh, you'll be okay," Elley calmly replied, hugging her. "It's only a little sledding accident."

That kid had no more than quieted down when a third one flung open the door and shouted, "Marieka is eating frozen pony turds. Yuk! Disgusting dog!"

"Did you ever try one?" Elley asked. "This is one of Marieka's favorite winter pastimes. She plays with them a lot. Let's everyone go 'yuk' together, on the count of three. One-two-three! Yuuuuuuk, disgusting dog!"

What a great way to live, I thought, as I watched the scenario. The only way you can tell the adults from the kids is by size. They play together. They work together. And they stay together, something this country needs more of.

"Do you like turkey?" Elley called to me over the commotion. "Mark, who lives at the next house up the hill, is cooking a community feed, and you're invited. He caretakes the home he's staying in. He's not an actual land-trust member; he's from Massachusetts. We call him an honorary creep. These are his girlfriend Dora's kids. They're visiting from Solon, today."

"Come on," Elley said to Ethan, who was entertaining Dora's now-giggling girls in the living room. "Let's go up to Mark's for dinner."

With Elley leading the way, we filed out the door and followed a footpath through the woods a short distance to Mark's house. Trooping into the kitchen, we found Mark sliding a huge turkey out of the oven.

Mark looked like Paul Bunyan: black-bearded, tall, and muscular. He was wearing blue jeans that were too short and exposed white socks above his boot tops. With a butcher knife in his right hand, he sliced the tender turkey. On the counter sat steaming bowls of peas, squash, mashed potatoes, and stuffing. His mother's homemade bread and several pies for dessert completed the menu.

While he stirred the gravy, Mark told me, "This backwoods country is great. While I'm cooking, I watch the deer or moose in the backyard. I feed the squirrels and birds. That's why I live in Creep City."

"How'd you come by the name Creep City?" I asked.

"We named the community in honor of the first child born here, Joshua. He used to call everybody "Queeps." Elley, helping set the table, spoke up. "Its legal name is Land Trust Number 45. We're on the forty-fifth parallel. There are twenty of us in the Land Trust. Three families are full-time: Richard and Martha, myself and Ethan, and Jack and Linda Hilmer and their crew. Jack cuts wood. Linda is pretty much a homemaker. Then there are four or five part-time winter families. And, let's see, there are one, two, three...four snowbirds--families that are here in the summer and gone in the winter. It gets too cold and they head out."

"How long have you been here?"

"I moved here in 1976. When we first started the Land Trust back in 1975, I made up my mind to live here year-round. You know, there's a book titled, *We Took to the Woods*. It's a book about a family who moved to the forest to get away from it all, Louise Dickinson Rich wrote it.

"Yes, I've read it," I said.

"Well, it about sums up our way of life. She wrote:
"I know that many people — perhaps most people — couldn't feel that, living here, they held within their grasp all the best in life. So for them it wouldn't be the best. For us, it is."

Creep City was another step in my growth. I found peace here. I found a community of people who were bound by a common thread. They were a close-knit group. They lived in close proximity. They lived close to the earth. They shared the same ideals, and they shared many of the same goals. These were a people who lived life for what it gave them. They were hard working, fun loving, and they graciously accepted whatever hand life dealt.

They reminded me of the people in the town of Buxton, during the years when I grew up. Like it or not, what you saw was what you got. I respected that. And the kids, sliding in their stainless steel mixing bowls, reminded me of my youth. In flying saucers, we kids, hooting, hollering, and screaming, used to slide down Mickey Moulton's and Clyde Harmon's farm fields. We had a grand old time.

Back in 1967, my senior year in high school, one of Clyde's employees said of me, "I hate to see Charlie go to Vietnam. He's a nervous sort. He'll probably never come home." Well, I did come home, at least physically. One of my friend's sons, who is now in Korea, recently wrote home to his mom,

"I now at least partially understand daddy a little bit. When he came home from work he was there, but he wasn't. He was home, but at the same time he was someplace else. It was like he was in another world. I haven't gone through anything like what daddy did, but I understand a little bit better. Now I know why he wasn't there. Tell him I love him."

Thinking of all these things and talking into a tape recorder as I drove up Creep City's road made for a pensive drive. I stopped to see Bruce on my way home and Noreen was there. She said, with a warm smile, "I was hoping you'd stop by on your way out. I want to tell you something: Even though this country didn't see fit to welcome you boys home, the patriotic people do care, do understand, and love you for what you did, for how you served. It's because of soldiers like you, and Bruce, and all the others that we enjoy our freedom, that Creep City can be Creep City." And she vigorously shook my hand.

I couldn't respond, didn't need to. There was nothing more to be said. I just turned, stepped into Festus, broke down, and headed home. All I could think of on my way home was a letter my parents received from the Department of the Army. It informed them that I had been assigned to Company A, 62nd Engineer Battalion in Vietnam. There was another letter I received from then Governor Ken Curtis that welcomed me home from Vietnam. Even though it was a form letter, he personally signed it. And though I have never met the man, I love and respect him for it.

Creep City is still much the same as it was. Some of the faces have changed, but nothing else.

(Creep City Crew at Parting.)

Chapter Five
Grand Isle
Rose

It was one o'clock on a blisteringly hot July afternoon when I met Rose.

Knocking on the front door of her house in Grand Isle, then peering through the window in the door, I could see her craning her neck to look at me over her shoulder. She was standing sideways in her bare feet between the kitchen-sink cabinet and a gas oven, peeling potatoes and dropping the peelings into a five-gallon bucket. As soon as her hands were free, she waved for me to come in.

(Rose's Kitchen, Grand Isle)

She looked to be in her early forties. Her trim figure was nicely outlined by skintight jeans. Her upper body was clad in a loose white sweatshirt with "U.S.A." emblazoned in red and blue on the left sleeve. Shoulder-length ebony hair framed her bronzed, Indian-brown face. Her deep brown eyes sparkled like a tantalizing deer's in the night and her teeth were as white as the driven snow.

In short, she was incredibly beautiful. If she hadn't been Miss Universe yet, she should have been. There wasn't any room here for Vietnam to invade my thoughts.

"Good afternoon," she said as calmly as if she had known me all her life. "Please, come in."

"Thank you."

I set my camera and tape recorder down on the kitchen table and introduced myself, somewhat baffled by her openness toward a man she had never met. Wow, I thought, she's not only beautiful, she's friendly.

"Charlie. I like that," she said, as she just started right in talking. "It's a calm name, a lot nicer than Charles or Chuck. Mom always called me Rosebud. My grandmother wanted to call me Butterball because, as a child, I was short and fat. Mom said that wasn't a good name for a girl to be raised with, so they settled on Rosebud. My real name is Esquaree, but everyone calls me Rose."

She wiped her hands on a dish towel, tossed it on the side of the sink, and then walked over to shake my hand. Shaking her hand, and trying to get my wits about me, I didn't quite know what to say, so I explained what I was doing.

"You have a good aura, you know. Some people I wouldn't have invited in. Now tell me how you found me."

"I stopped in Van Buren and asked Pete Ashley if he

knew of anyone living back in the woods," I answered. "Pete's a schoolteacher I knew in high school. I had already interviewed as many non-native Mainers as I needed, but then Pete told me about you. He said you moved up from Harlem and had accomplished a lot here. He was really impressed. He told me about your 'No Trespassing' sign, too, but he said it was mostly for hunters. He didn't think you'd mind if I came up."

"Yeah, he's pretty much right," she deadpanned. "I just don't want a bunch of people coming up here hunting or looking around or whatever. The people I don't like are all buried out back. If it's winter, I just keep them cold in the snow till spring."

Then she cracked another smile, we both laughed, and she continued, "What Mr. Ashley said was nice. I know who he is—in a small town, everybody knows everybody. I have a dog-grooming business in Van Buren. I either met him there or maybe at the school. I took some Adult Ed classes my first two years here. Back then I was living on the money I saved in New York and I didn't have to work."

Excusing herself, Rose went into the living room and returned with a report card from Van Buren High School. "Hot damn," she said, handing me the card and sitting back down. "I completed both of these courses."

One course was in small-engine repair and the other was in welding.

It didn't take an imagination to see how proud Rose was. I was still amazed at her openness with me. She treated me like her long lost brother.

Grinning broadly, she tapped her fingers on the table, anxious for my response to her report card. "This is terrific," I said, holding up the card. "You should really be proud."

"It's super neat," Rose said. "Mom was quite happy, too. I proved I can take care of myself. I've lived here for ten years now, since I was thirty-one. I haven't been back home for more than five years. I hate going back, even though my family's there. It's been six or seven years since Mom and my sister came up. When they did, they were surprised. Mom thought I'd be living in an eight-by-eight cabin or something. She was delighted. Now she tells everyone how wonderful my home is."

Rose's house was about two miles into the woods and sat high up on a hill overlooking Route 1 in Aroostook County, virtually in the shadow of the Canadian Mountains. The house was a log cabin in the truest sense, with logs varying in size. The outside was weathered to a natural gray from years of exposure.

Rose leaned back in the chair and cupped her hands behind her head. "I love it," she said. "I like the natural weathered look of the full round logs. This isn't one of those commercial pseudo-log homes with flat inside walls. This is right off the land; yeah, it really makes me feel much closer to nature.

"I can't ever see myself leaving," Rose said, toying with her hair as she spoke. "Mom had problems with me the whole time I was growing up. She wanted me to marry a rich man. I was a tomboy with skinned knees and scars and always doing the opposite of what Mom thought I should be doing. I kept toilets running and the window shades operating — I kept everything working. 'Wait a minute, Mom,' I told her. 'You can't have both. Do you want your toilets working or me wiggling my butt around for the guys?' I could have had any guy I wanted, but all I wanted was out of New York."

"My sister is borderline retarded," she said. "So after I got her settled in a shelter-type home, I left New York. I was gone like a big bird."

"You know, I hated winter in New York. The last place I thought I'd move would be Maine. But when a friend showed me an ad for this place in *Mother Earth News* — it was beautiful, just beautiful. My brother and I took a ride up. I fell in love with it, bought it, and moved up two years later."

"I was raised in Harlem, like Mr. Ashley told you. But I lived on Staten Island for many years before I moved here. One place wasn't much different from another; it was definitely less than desirable, both on the streets and at home."

Rose excused herself and returned with a map of New York. Sitting beside me now, she spread the map out on the table, took my pen, and said, pointing, "The Big Apple. This is where I lived."

"I don't wonder you wanted to get out of there," I said, looking at Rose. "I could never live in a city, especially a city as big as New York. What you've done here is quite impressive. You've broken the clutch that seems to hold people who live in depressed regions of huge cities."

"Most people do have a hard time moving away from where they grew up," she said. "They don't know there are alternatives. If they do know, most don't have what it takes to pick up and move. My brother talks about leaving New York, but spends all his money on expensive things for his home."

"I was fortunate. I was shown an alternative and did something about it," Rose said. "It was like...serendipity."

She stood and walked to the living-room window, where I joined her. We looked beyond the field of daisies, beyond the St. John River and into New Brunswick, Canada. We watched and heard the train clackety-clack by, running parallel to the logging trucks as they jostled along the old dirt road on the Canadian side of the river. Standing there, Rose was confident, completely at ease, and her gentle manner also put me at ease. I was relaxed and felt good.

"When I was fourteen," Rose said, "I went to a Catholic school for six or eight weeks in the Pocono Mountains. They had log cabins and a big lodge, and oh, I liked that, I really did. That's when my love for the country began."

"When I left the Poconos, my mother sent me to a boarding school in Peekskill, New York. I was there for a year and a half. It was actually like a sentence, so I was looking for an out. Then I started going with this fellow, Johnny, when I was sixteen. He talked about buying an island and raising a family. You know, the whole romantic picture. That's when I really started saving. I could see real possibilities. I went with him for thirteen years, till I was twenty-nine. But he couldn't save, and I could. So we drifted like that train." Rose pointed to the end of the train as it passed from sight.

"I traded my old life for a better one," she said. "I saved so much and was so tight with my money, my mother accused me of squeezing a nickel so hard, I made the buffalo poop. She told me, 'Your frugality is in your Scottish and Dutch blood. It's not in your father's Cherokee or Mohawk, and it's not in Mother's Barbados blood either.' I didn't care whose blood my frugality came from. I figured I'd sooner go without for a short time to get something I really wanted. I'd still be in New York if I hadn't saved."

"Would you like a drink of cold well water?" Rose asked. She grabbed a five-gallon bucket, handed me two glasses, and walked out the door to a nearby water pump.

"You know, the drive up here is some kind of pretty," I said. "The dirt road was a bit bumpy, but once I got into the fields where it's been bulldozed, it was a pleasant drive. The fields are alive with white and blue wildflowers. A couple of rabbits were bounding around and yellow buttercups were dancing in the warm breeze."

"Yes, it is nice. It's always nice," Rose replied, pumping on the handle to fill the glasses I held. "Wallace bulldozed my driveway for me. He's a friend from town. The driveway is just a narrow place plowed up through the field. It gets terribly muddy. I can't use it in the rain. I can't use it in the winter, either."

"You know, it's the view of the Canadian mountains that I like the best. From up here, they have a blue hue like the mountains in Virginia. I just love it. It's private, too."

The twinkle in her eye made me wonder what she was going to say next.

"It's my little sanctuary," she said. "Sometimes, I run out of the house bare-ass naked. It's like a whole different freedom. I run out and get the wood or go to the barn, summer and winter. Well, in the winter, it's a quick trip."

"I'd like to have a pond up here, and a sauna." Rose said. "You'd be a nice prospect to share that with." She had the same twinkle in her eye. "Few people understand how to really enjoy the outdoors. They make something bad out of something good. If you live with it, nature is wonderfully fun and interesting!"

"Do you use this snowplow?" I asked, changing the subject and hoping she wouldn't see my face turning red. I walked toward the old International snowplow parked on her front lawn. This part of her property reminded me of what I thought Harlem might look like. Parked side-by-side next to the snowplow, she had a Ford pickup, a Pontiac, a Plymouth, and two Mustangs, all but one in sad condition. Closer to the barn, I saw eight different snowmobiles, lined up one behind the other like the cars of a train.

"I've used all these cars and snowmobiles at one time or another," Rose said, as she walked past the snowplow and the cars to the snowmobiles. She sat on a Cobra and offered me the Polaris, facing her.

"I didn't start buying snowmobiles until I'd been here a while. When I first moved in, I skied and snow-shoed the two miles down to Route 1, carrying a kerosene lantern. I only went out every three weeks to get my mail and pick up supplies. I used to get sixty pounds of sugar 'cause I drank a lot of Kool-Aid, a case of toilet paper, fifty pounds of flour, a case of canned milk, twenty pounds of spaghetti, ten pounds of dried beans, fifteen pounds of tuna, a hundred pounds of cat food, three hundred pounds of dog food, duck food, pony grain, hay, and all kinds of stuff like that."

She had a unique way of hauling in supplies. She built a high-sided wagon on skis.

"I had all that animal food," she continued, "because I had a lot of critters from New York. They were old when I moved here, though, and they died off. My white duck was my buddy. I'd call him by name and he'd come running. I got him a little pencil-colored duck so he'd have a wife, and they had kids. "A motley bunch," she added. "I named my duck Davy, after my boss in New York, because he was pigeon-toed and bald-headed." Rose rotated her toes in against the Cobra and pulled her hair back with the fingers of both hands, like she was bald.

"I hauled my supplies in that way for more than a year,"

Rose said, returning to our earlier discussion, "until I bought that snowmobile sitting way back there." She pointed to the last sled in the row. "When I got back from town with my groceries and mail, I'd ski the two miles back up from Route 1 and get Shazba, my pony. Then I'd walk back down with him harnessed to the sled, load the groceries, and he'd pull them back up. That was eight miles every three weeks or so. It was so nice 'cause it would be twilight when I finished and I'd hear the coyotes. At first I was afraid. But I'd look at Shazba and if he wasn't reacting, then I figured it was safe. When I went to hauling with the skidoo, it kind of lost something, some of the romance."

(Rose's Horse, Shazba.)

Rose called every snowmobile she had a skidoo. It didn't matter what brand it was.

"Now I don't shop that way because I go out four or five days a week. When I get out to Route 1, I need a car. That Mustang over by the snowplow," Rose nodded toward the car, "I bought when I first moved here. My brother showed me how to work on cars when I was back in New York, so I never minded owning one."

"I learned everything hands-on. Everything was really hit or miss," she said, extending her arms, with upturned palms. Her hands were dainty like a woman's, yet also tough-looking like a man's.

"What I didn't learn from my brother, I learned in Adult-Ed classes. I took small-engine repair, snowmobile repair, welding, and carpentry. If I didn't keep things going, I had to walk; so I made it my business to keep things going. That's why I have so many cars and snowmobiles. When one breaks, I use it for spare parts to fix another."

(Rose's Cabin in Grand Isle.)

"See that cleated ramp going up onto my porch?" Rose said, pointing toward the cabin. "I built that so I can work on my snowmobiles in the house. I get oil all over the kitchen floor. But I can tear one apart, rebuild it from other carburetors, and have a machine going in twenty minutes."

"And that firewood you see stacked beside the house," Rose nodded in the direction of her woodpile, "I cut and split it myself. I bought a chain saw when I first moved here."

Rose's woodpile was stacked in an open-sided, roofed lean-to. From years of heaving in the frost, the roof bellied like a sway-back horse. But the wood was piled high, followed the roof line, and was stacked with the care of an artist. No stick was protruding farther than another.

"The first three years I cut it off my land," Rose said. "Now I have eight-foot bolts delivered. But that first year I was cutting bolts bigger than me and lugging them out on my back. I lugged a cord and a half that way, until I had big bulges on my shoulders. I said, 'I'm gonna kill myself doing this.' Then I thought of Shazba. He likes to pull, so I hooked him up and for the next three years, he twitched[1] all my wood. He was a real lifesaver. But then one day he got in an accident and impaled himself with a broken sapling. That was the last time he twitched wood. It took him almost three years to heal. I thought I was going to lose my buddy."

Rose got up and I followed her down a path to a cedar-shingled barn. Among other things, it was filled with acetylene tanks and torches, bush cutters, handsaws, chainsaws, hammers, wrenches, screwdrivers, grain, and hay. The only empty spot in the barn was the pony's stall.

---

[1] Twitched: a woodcutter's term for moving logs from the place where they are cut.

79

Hidden in the hardwoods like it was, the barn looked like an old western line shack with a stick corral. The pony had been grazing, but when he saw Rose, he came running and stuck his head over the fence, nudging her shoulder.

"He's only been in a fence for a couple weeks now. After he hurt himself, I let him run loose. But he was amusing himself by eating the beans I'd planted on the side of the house. I said, 'Guess what? Your butt is going in the corral 'cause you ate my beans.' He's twenty-three. He's so funny. He really loves marshmallows. He'll follow me up the ramp to the house and look in the window for a bag of marshmallows."

"When I first moved here," she resumed, leaning into the fence and scratching the pony's forehead, "everyone downtown and in New York thought this was sheer folly, that I was out to lunch, some kind of crazy person. They said I couldn't do it."

"Everyone thought I needed a man. I had a boyfriend here for a while, but I shipped him out. Now, maybe I'm going with Wallace, maybe I'm not. I love living alone. It gets real comfortable. You have so much freedom. You don't have to worry about somebody else. Who needs a man when you can go to bed with a good book?"

"Don't get me wrong," Rose said, as she patted the pony's back. "I'm not saying we don't all need help now and then. I'm just saying I like living alone. Wallace has helped me a lot. But other people have too. Mr. Morrow from down the road let me use his welder. The posts under my house were rotten, so I borrowed his welder and some jacks, and we put L-shaped beams under the house and welded iron posts to them. Mr. Morrow and my neighbor, Jim Callahan, helped me put the new roof up. The original roof was log rafters. It rotted so bad the eaves fell off. Every time it rained I had puddles all over the house. It was getting to be a downright emergency. When we put the new roof on, we went with two-by-six rafters on log purloins that run lengthwise."

We walked back toward the house. "My fancy outhouse," Rose said as we passed by. "The roof caved in this past winter. And it's starting to lean. I'm gonna have to build a new one."

I opened the door to take a look.

"Do it pretty quick, I'd say. If you ain't careful, you're gonna fall in."

We stepped onto the porch, which looked like a greenhouse of hanging plants.

"People were somewhat right when they figured I couldn't handle the isolation and the snow," Rose admitted. "There is a line you know, a line of terror. When I first moved here, I was terrified of the snow. I thought when I stepped in it, I'd sink to my eyebrows. It didn't occur to me that I couldn't sink any deeper than the snow was. Then one night we had thirty-nine inches and I had an appointment in town the next day. When I got up, I said, 'Oh my God, what do people do with all this snow?' I was terrified. But I skied down to my car anyway. The whole two miles down to Route 1, my eyelashes kept freezing together, and I had to keep rubbing my eyes so I could see. But it was a winter wonderland. The snow glistened on the trees and bushes, almost like glass. Now winter is my favorite time of year."

Following Rose into the house, I sat at the table while she turned on the gas stove. "We'll have some hot chocolate, soon as the water heats," she said. "I didn't make a mistake coming up here, for sure," Rose continued, standing by the stove. "The people here, by and large, are good people; there's no two ways about it. In New York, you don't know if the face you're looking at is good or bad. Being there gives you a bad attitude. Here it's a small town. You know the rotten people."

"I got to know people around here quite good from my work. After I'd been here a couple of years, I found out that money doesn't keep," Rose said, setting down two mugs of steaming hot chocolate. "So I went to work at the Presque Isle Animal Hospital, grooming dogs. Now I work four days a week at my own shop in Van Buren. It gives me an income, but it also takes me away from home. And here, right here, is my idea of relaxation. I love my work; it's just that sometimes people have ridiculous demands. But it's nothing like the rat race in New York. Living here is my sense of accomplishment."

Looking around Rose's house, everything I saw spoke eloquently of accomplishment. Her home told a story louder than words ever could about a proud, yet humble, independent woman. Her neatly kept library covered an entire living-room wall. Books lined the shelves from floor to ceiling. Two shelves heavy with smaller books were placed below a small window. Sunlight streamed through the uppermost panes, casting a long shadow from the schoolboy-type desk midway in the room across the pine board floor. The ceilings, like the floors, were also pine board. They were nailed to huge, open timbers.

Between the library and the kitchen was a rustic log stairway, with a record cabinet built under the lower portion. I followed Rose up the stairs. Her bedroom was as neat as the rest of the house. Under the bed were built-in drawers for clothes.

(Rose's Library in Grand Isle.)

She looked at me and said, "This is nice up here. It's cozy. I lie in bed at night and dream. I can look right into Canada."

Downstairs, Rose's house was one big open room. A Crawley-800 woodstove with a black pan simmering on top for humidity sat opposite the stairs, adjacent to the kitchen sink.

"None of these furnishings you see are new." She said. "I brought them all up from New York. The only thing that's new is this."

She bent over between the stove and the stairs to lift up a trap door. "It's my refrigerator. Wallace built it for me. It's just a metal box set in the floor. But it keeps things cooler. Canned goods that don't need refrigeration I keep over there," she said, pointing to the shelves beside the table."

(Rose Standing in her Front Door.)

Sitting at the table, I asked Rose how she operates her record player.

"I use twelve-volt batteries," she said. "But they're awful. Every time I go downtown to get them recharged, the battery acid burns holes in my clothes." She held her sweatshirt out for me to see. "I have them charged a couple times a month. They run my TV and VCR, too. I hope to put solar in this year. I have the stuff. I just haven't gotten around to it. When I do, I'll use it for lights, too. Right now I use gas and candles, and a Coleman light sometimes."

Above Rose's table hung a gaslight. Another one was in the living room by her library; still another was over the kitchen sink, where she took her baths. "My mother asked me how I take a bath in that sink. I told her, 'As long as you can get your butt in, you can take a bath.'"

"You know," Rose said, as we walked out to Festus, "right over there by my well pump, two deer keep coming out of the woods. One time, I just lay down and froze, watching them. They came within fifteen feet of me, sniffing. I'm sure they would have sniffed my feet if someone coming up from the field hadn't startled them. Now I stalk deer. It's a blast. But that first time, I was floating off the ground, I was so excited."

Just then the train whistled as it came through the pass, heading south toward Van Buren. The sun was getting low when I started Festus. I rolled the window down and shook Rose's hand. Then she pointed to the sun as it settled below the distant Canadian hills, casting the last rays of the day. With the now-familiar twinkle in her eye, she turned to me and said, "The sunsets are always special here."

Rose was a rare individual. From her, I learned a great deal about letting go. She didn't live in the past; instead, she lived in the now and prepared for the future. It took over six hours to drive from Rose's house to my house. I got home late and was very tired. But the next day, I went to church in Bangor and met a new Bishop who helped me start making some important changes in my life.

(Grand Isle -- Snowmobiles and Cars)

Chapter Six
On the Canadian Border
Spirit and Faith

Three hours north of Canaan, I stopped at one of those poke and plumb towns, where if you poke your head out the window you're plumb out of town. This town's right on the Canadian border; actually it's the US Customs checkpoint. It was snowing and blowing and freezing cold when I stopped there at Labonte's Store.

"I think I'm lost," I said as I entered the store, hunching my shoulders at the sound of the door slamming behind me.

"Well, you must be, to end up in this small town," said Colette Labonte, a tall, slim woman, bagging groceries for a customer.

Labonte's was the last store on Route 27 before entering Canada on the Western border with Maine. It was an original, backcountry, if we-ain't-got-it, you-don't-need-it store. Ice-fishing traps, scoops, and augers hung on the walls, and the aisles were stacked with flour, sugar, vegetables, and almost anything else you can find in a supermarket.

Wiping her hands on her apron, Colette asked, "What are you doing up here?"

"I'm hunting for a guy by the name of John Latwin," I said. "Sorry about the door."

Reaching out to shake my hand, she said, "That's okay, we're used to it. You must be the writer. John said someone like you might be looking for him."

"How did he know about me?"

"John came out last night and went to Trail's End in Eustis," she said. "He stopped here to pick up a few things on his way home and told us that the Copelans, who own Trail's End, had given you his name yesterday. You're lucky! The man doesn't entertain much company, and he doesn't come out very often. But he said if you came, call him on the crank phone and he would come out and get you on his snowmobile."

"I'll get my husband," Collette said. "He's out pumping gas. His name is John, too. He'll take you to the crank phone, if I can't reach Griz on the regular phone. Everyone around here calls him Grizzly Adams."

When Colette couldn't reach Griz on the cellular phone, it took only a couple of minutes for her husband and me to walk the quarter length of town to the gatekeeper's log cabin, where the crank phone was located. John Labonte stood over six feet tall. He was thin-faced and rugged. He was wearing heavy wool clothing and black gloves, and packs on his feet. We both had our hoods up trying to protect our ears from the cold wind. We stepped through an opening where a screened porch door used to be and into a three-foot entryway of the log cabin. More appropriately it might be referred to as a line shack from a Louis L'Amour western. I noticed an old wooden box hanging on the wall with a crank phone in it. A faded white poster to the left of the phone read "DUFFY'S DEER YARD."

John said, "In the summer months, a gate-tender lives here and doesn't let anyone on this logging road who doesn't belong."

Grabbing the phone handle, John gave it one long crank and two shorts.

"Hello," he said. "This is the other John. There's a guy

down here looking for you." There was a short pause, than he hung up.

(Duffy's Deer Yard Crank Phone to Big Island Pond Camps.)

"Drive up this road seven miles until you come to Griz's truck," John said. "He'll be waiting for you."

Once back in Festus, I looked just beyond the cabin at a sign painted in three-inch, fire-engine-red letters, that read:

WARNING
This Is Not A
Snowmobile Trail
Plows And Equipment
May Be On Road
At Any Time

(It's a long way from Coburn Gore to John Latwin's.)

The un-kept, roller-coaster road wound through the border mountains, tunneling along under a canopy of freezing, cracking limbs. Two-foot snowdrifts covered the road where the dense, intermittent soft- and hard-wood forest opened, allowing the cold December winds through. The spruce, fir, and hardwoods swayed from the force of the northerly winds. The smaller coniferous trees shuddered in the bitter cold. Their limbs sprang up, relieved after the wind shook heavy snow off their branches.

My two-wheel-drive Toyota labored as it plowed through snowdrifts and past a five-acre bog nestled in a pocket of low rolling mountains.

I had driven four miles when the forest closed in again. Three more miles and someone who could only be John Latwin was riding up the road on a snowmobile and stopped where his truck was parked. A galvanized tin box rested on the back of an iron-skied sleigh that tagged along behind.

After he stopped, John stood beside his snowmobile. He looked to be an inch or two over six feet. His long silver hair and beard flowed in the wind, while his penetrating blue eyes bore down on me like the scope of a long-range rifle. He was wearing an elegant foxtail hat, foot-long beaver-pelt mittens, felt-lined boots, a snowmobile suit, and a green-and-black-checkered wool jacket with a Maine guide patch on the right sleeve.

Smiling, he shook my right hand with a vise-like grip and introduced himself, asking if I had any trouble driving up.

"No," I said, trying to spread my fingers apart after he let go.

"Throw your gear in the gray box," he said. "It's too cold to stand around here jawin'. But before we go, you have to promise not to mention this lake or the town down the mountain by name. I don't want people knowin' where I'm at."

After promising not to mention the town by name, I pulled my face mask on and we were off. John only knew one speed — fast! The trees were a blur as we sped along the first three miles to the lake.

I kept my head bowed behind John's back so the wind wouldn't freeze my face during the five-mile ride. Approaching the lake, we were traveling so fast that we missed the usual entrance, plowing through a three-foot snowdrift. Midway across the lake, John stopped and pointed out each surrounding mountain.

"Beautiful, isn't it." He said. It was a statement, not a question and he stretched his arms up toward the mountain summits like Moses parting the Red Sea.

The word "beautiful," I thought, lacked the elegance of

expression that this place deserved. "Yes, it is, John," I replied. "But somehow it's more than that."

Towering mountains surrounded the lake. Their frosty, snowcapped summits seemed to melt away to the holiday green of the conifers below. Farther down, naked hardwoods intermixed with the evergreens that lined the lake's shore.

(The U.S.-Canadian Border from Big Island Pond.)

"Look yonder," John said, pointing. "The tops of them mountains is the Canadian border. There are many old trails weaving through them hills. The mail used to be delivered on foot to the people who lived back here. Now I have to skidoo five miles, and drive about thirty, to pick up my mail in Eustis. I don't go out more than once a week. I hate to leave the mountains."

(John Latwin, Trapper, Big Island Pond Camps Caretaker.)

Snowflakes stung my eyes as we sped across the last mile of the rough, snow-drifted lake. Traveling up the shoreline, we wove in and out, dodging trees and boulders as we made our way to John's cabin.

The cabin sat back from the lake on a knoll nestled in a grove of firs. It was constructed of chinked logs and had four rooms and a loft. The kitchen had an old gas stove, oven, and refrigerator along one wall. On the wall overlooking the lake was a long black-slate sink, resting on a cabinet base under a large window. An old water pump was set on the boarded countertop at the right end of the sink. The other two walls were covered with cabinets and shelves, and a gas hot-water heater in one corner supplied warm water for the shower.

Under the living-room floor, John had a root cellar where he kept the winter food supply. The living room had three

93

log walls and one wall with knotty-pine paneling. Gaslights, fish-species maps, topographical maps, coyote pelts, a beaver pelt, a fly-fishing rod, and various garments hung on the walls.

The floor was buried under two feet of books, maps, pelts, cans of hide-tanning solution, traps, and everything else imaginable. We had to move things around so I could sit down.

"Don't mind the junk," John said. "I pick it up in the spring."

By the looks, he hadn't picked it up any sooner than spring. The floor wasn't visible anywhere.

I tiptoed around, helping him move things, hoping I wouldn't step on anything valuable, like one of his beaver or coyote skulls. Chuckling at the mess I had just walked through, I finally slid a chair up to the table and was happy to sit where it was warm.

John was anxious to talk. "My root cellar is under that clutter, over there somewhere."

"Oh," I said, smiling. "Do you buy much food?"

"I buy taters by the hundred-weight, vegetables by the case, and store them in the root cellar. I keep my meat in a friend's freezer down the mountain. I got me a deer, twenty partridge, and some beaver liver too. That beaver liver is the best I've ever eaten," John said, licking his lips. "You ever had any?"

"Nope. I've had enough deer steak to make up for it, though. Do you usually get a deer? I noticed you've got some horns lying around."

"Every year. I shot my last deer thirteen times, boom, boom, boom, with a 308," John said, standing and holding his arms up as if aiming a rifle. "I knocked him ass over bandbox with my first three shots. The son of a bitch got up and ran right by me."

John reminded me of Bub Dow, an old guide and trapper who used to hunt with me. I didn't think anyone could spin yarns like Bub, but John was giving him a run for his money. John embellished his stories with various mannerisms, boom-boom-booms, and an Allagash twang.

It was obvious that he was trying to fill me full of it. He loved telling stories to anyone who would listen, and hoped to be included in my book, as he asked, "You mean I might get in your book?"

"I shot him again," John continued, deep into his story about the buck. "Boom-boom-boom-boom. He ran about fifty feet and got in with some does. When the does ran, I got another good shot. This time I shot him three more times, boom-boom-boom." John swung around, aiming out the window. "He fell and got right back up, standin' in a brook, so I shot him three more times, boom-boom-boom. That was it. It was the end of the chase. He fell deader than a nit. He weighed 205 pounds and had ten points. I hit him in the chest right where I aimed," John said, pointing at his own chest, "All thirteen times. You could have covered the hole with a beaver's nut."

No wonder John's deer are so heavy, I thought, with all that lead in them.

"I get big bucks every year," John said, interrupting my thoughts. "It just happens that way. Boom-boom. I just seem to get them. I think I'm a big buck hunter. I get big coyotes, too. See that big one over yonder?" John asked, pointing at his pelts. "He was big enough to be a wolf."

"I only trap for my own use, ya know. I don't want to exploit them. I only want to make my clothin'. I don't trap much.

"I'm makin' a coyote coat now. Most all winter, I tie flies for Pines Market and some other stores in the area. In the summer I guide fishin'."

Besides fly-tying, John's been a logger, trapper, and caretaker of sporting camps. He was born and raised in the North Woods of Maine. His father worked in the woods, too. It's the only life he has ever known, and the only one he wants to know.

"Say! You ain't seen my new bucket-flush commode yet," he said. "Yup, last summer I put her in. She's over there, behind that wall with the pelts on it."

As I walked over to see the bathroom, John raised his voice and kept on talking. "I had an outhouse for years; fact is, I've still got it. I just don't use it anymore. It's too blamed cold out there. I used to bring my toilet seat in from the outhouse at night and keep it warm behind the stove. That helped. But when it was stormin' out, bringin' in the seat didn't do any good," John hollered, to make sure I heard him, "so, I'd shit on a newspaper and burn it. That beat the hell out of freezin' my ass off."

"You know," John continued, as I slid my chair back up to the table, "everyone down the mountain calls me Grizzly Adams. I figure what they mean is, I'm a real backwoodsman. Livin' up here made me appreciate the others that live in the forest.

"I sit in this cozy cabin, cookin' my supper, but you take that coyote over there, that son of a bitch, every night he sleeps out in the cold. He lives out there. I have five coyote packs around. They all get howlin' back and forth at night. They have a regular chorus. Then I get to feed the Gorbies. Come outside a minute, I'll show you. You watch, they'll fly down, land on my fingertips, and peck the bread out of my hand."

Standing outside, I watched as John held out a handful of bread crumbs. The Canadian Jays swooped down, lighted on his fingertips, pecked at the bread, then flew off to store it and returned for more. "Haw! Haw! Haw!" John laughed. "This place floats my boat. I've got a bunch of grosbeaks and chickadees, too."

(John Latwin Feeding a Gorby Bird.)

Back inside, John continued, "At night I'll go out, listen to the owls and coyotes and watch the stars."

Suddenly, I thought how lucky we are to live in a country where the stars aren't exploding all around, like the rockets in Vietnam. Here in the Maine woods the stars are like huge glittering candles — they're peaceful and tranquil. Often in Vietnam the skies were tense and filled with death. The tracer rounds from M-60 machine guns, M-16 rifles, M-14 rifles, and chopper fire, crisscrossed in every direction, and filled the skies with thousands of orange and red streaks that sped along, seemingly with the speed of shooting stars.

"Hey, you were off in another world," John spoke, waving his hand in front of my face, bringing me out of my trance. "Are you okay? You're a bit teary eyed. You live some bad memories don't you? You're even shaking."

"I'm sorry, John," I said, completely embarrassed. "Sometimes people say things, or I see something that triggers, yes, John, you said it, 'bad memories.'"

"I didn't mean to say somethin'…"

"It's okay, John. It isn't you," I interrupted. "It just happens now and then."

John wanted me to know that things weren't always as romantic as they seemed where he lived either. To try to ease things up, he said, "Sometimes things can get mighty rough up here, too. A man has to know what he's doin'."

Bringing a friend out to visit during a heavy snowstorm a few years back, John got in trouble. The outboard motor on his pontoon raft stopped running when they were only halfway across the lake, and then the only paddle broke. Deep slush built up, stranding them a hundred feet from shore.

"There we were," John said, "huddled under a tarp until two in the mornin'."

That was when game wardens showed up in a canoe.

The Labontes had called John at seven that evening, wondering why he hadn't brought his friend back out. When there was no answer, they knew something was wrong and notified the wardens.

"If it hadn't been for those wardens, I'd be dead," John

said. "Before morning, the lake froze solid. I walked out on the ice and got my things off the raft. I had to leave the raft in all winter. I've got a lot of respect for those wardens now. They've got a tough job. I used to do a few things I shouldn't. I don't no more."

"Folks talked about that out to town for a spell, but I don't care what happens outside, and I have no desire to live there. I go to town and people ask if I heard about this or that. I tell them no, I didn't hear about nothin'," John said, cackling. "Town folks ask if I get lonely. 'Lonely for what?' I ask. I've lived like this most of my life. I've got everything I want or need."

John jumped up to show me three newly tied flies. "Not many people can sit here and tie these all day. Then they ask if I get cabin fever. Bah, that's all in people's heads." John held up a fly and, pointing out the window, said, "See how those mountains rise into the sky? They're just like big tits. I love 'em. I feel fortunate livin' here. How many people are happy doing what they do? You don't hear me complainin'.

"Other people can't take a day off because they need every day's pay for a four-wheeler or some other damn thing. They waste money on things they really don't need and miss what really counts. They're missin' it all as far as I'm concerned."

Holding up a pendulum that he pulled out of his pocket, John said, "Most folks down the mountain don't believe in nothin' like this either. An Alaskan boy gave it to me when I went there pannin' gold last summer. Might like to live there sometime."

"The pendulum is made out of an empty rifle shell casing with this string tied through a hole drilled in the end," John explained. "Any shell casing will work. After looping the string around your index finger so the casing swings freely, you ask it yes and no questions. If it rotates in a large circle, then the answer to your question is yes. If it rotates in a small circle, the answer is no."

As an example, John asked if the ice was safe and if we would get out safely. The pendulum rotated in a big circle.

"There," John said, "there's your answer. You're going to get out safe. Ain't that somethin'? It don't work for everyone, but you try it."

I asked, "Will we see any coyote on the way out?" It rotated in a small circle.

(And, in fact, we didn't.)

We were going so fast across the lake and down the old road to the truck, we hardly saw anything except flying snow. The trip took us only five minutes, about a mile a minute. But John's speed didn't bother me. He was in his element, putting on a good show.

"Where ya headed next?" John asked as I started my Toyota.

"I don't know, John," I answered. "Up around Mount Katahdin, I guess. But don't ask me why, because I really don't know."

Shaking my hand, John said, as serious as I had seen him, "You take care. Try to learn not to let the past catch up with you. I know you know who Chief Joseph was. Do you remember what he said, 'From where the sun now stands, I will fight no more forever.' Let it go."

It was now John's eyes that were misty. He was talking to me like a father to a son. And though he never said it, the look he gave me told me he understood.

With vice-like grips we shook hands. We matched stares. And I knew that this man would always be a friend. John broke off the hand shake, and just as quick, spun around and left.

When he was fully out of sight I got back in my truck and left for home, thinking there's more to that man's life than he's willing to talk about. We had common ground. A common thread. Our spirits touched.

•••••

I sensed that I really needed to get religion back in my life, and keep it. My conscience was pricked by the caring spirits of these people like John Latwin. I needed the love, the closeness that came from people who cared. I hadn't been living the principles of the gospel of Jesus Christ. I had a lot of fences to mend. And so it was here, driving down these mountainous roads that I was able to follow up on my recent commitments to myself, put another chapter of Vietnam behind me, and decided to make sure I kept the promise I made to Heavenly Father in Vietnam — to go to church the rest of my life.

The next Sunday, once again, I found myself in the back pew at the Bangor Chapel of The Church of Jesus Christ of Latter-day Saints. It had been a long time since I been in church for two Sundays in a row and I still felt awkward. I wanted to get up and leave, but I remembered my promise to the bishop the previous Sunday. Looking up I recognized one of the men sitting on the stand: Bruce McLaughlin. He was an old friend. With a bit of an inquisitive look the man sitting beside Bruce on the stand looked at me. It was easy to see by the look in his eyes he was trying to figure out who I was. With his eyes locked on me he leaned over to Bruce and whispered in his ear. I could sense what he asked, and so knew he was the bishop. Even from the back row I could read Bruce's lips, "That's Charlie Reitze." They had a short conversation and opened the service. After the service this man who stood well over six feet came and greeted me. He was Bishop Lewis Hassell. He visited me at home. He visited me at church week after week. He interviewed me. We set goals. He cared. And I loved him for it.

I'm back now. I'm back from Vietnam. I'm back to church. I'm all the way back. I'm home.

I've never seen John Latwin since. He was the type of man who could disappear with the wind.

(On the Way to John Latwin's.)

Chapter Seven
Grand Lake Matagamon
The Guides

"The trapper?" the ranger at Chamberlain Lake asked, rubbing his jaw. "You're a mite late. He moved out ages ago. But if it's trappers you're looking for, why don't you go see Chub and Fran Foster? They live beyond Patten on the backshore of Grand Lake Matagamon. Chub's trapped all his life."

It was five p.m. when I started Festus and pulled out of the ranger station at Chamberlain Lake on my way to see the Fosters. The windshield was a rainbow of streaked ice from wipers trying to keep up with heavy snow.

Before me lay nearly a hundred and fifty miles, of which seventy were dirt roads owned by the paper company. This time of year they were glossy white with hard-packed, icy snow. The Pinkham Road was ten miles from the Chamberlain Lake ranger station; then Hey Pond, South Ridge, Middle Brook Mountain, South Lake, Hayden Brook, and Grove Hill took me another sixty miles to the small Aroostook town of Masardis, population 305. After stopping there for a hamburger and fries, both smothered in grease, I continued another forty miles past Pollard Mountain, Otter Pond, T7 R5, Mattawamkeag Hill, Halls Corner, Hersey, and Patten. From there, I drove another thirty miles out Route 159 and the Grand Lake Road, crossed Shin Pond Narrows, and passed Crommett Farm and Hey Lake to reach Grand Lake Matagamon.

(On the road to Grand Lake Matagamon.)

It was ten p.m. when I finally parked Festus in a snowplow turnaround at the point where the road closed for the winter. I set up my truck tent, lined my sleeping bag with my clothes, and climbed in, shivering and exhausted.

•••••

At seven in the morning, I eased my head out of the sleeping bag like a squirrel poking his head out of a tree. The morning sun had turned the frost on my tent to glistening crystals. So frigid was the air that I zipped the sleeping bag right back over me and dressed inside. The propane gas in my cook stove wouldn't work in the cold, so I started Festus. After the truck was warm enough, I fixed breakfast in the cab.

An hour later, it was time to start walking. The shadows of conifers were inching across the old road. Limbs were bent, touching the ground under the weight of a foot and a half of new snow. Hardwoods whipped back and forth in the wind, snapping like too-taut electrical wires. Bending over, I pulled the rubber snowshoe harnesses up around my sheepskin mukluks. Spitting the tail of my coonskin hat out of my mouth, I began a mile-long hike from where the snowplows stopped to the gate on the east side of Baxter State Park.

It was another three miles across Grand Lake Matagamon to Chub and Fran's house. Standing at the gate and looking across the windswept lake, I could barely see the cabin on the far side. They have to be home, I thought, but there was no visible smoke from the distant chimney. That didn't matter; I had made up my mind to go smoke or no smoke. I broke through a six-foot snowdrift and scuffed my way down onto the lake. Even though it was a brutally cold day—so cold my eyelashes were freezing—I was having the time of my life. In Vietnam I swore that I'd never complain of the cold again, and I wasn't about to; this was my kind of livin'.

Even halfway across the lake, with snow spirits swirling around me like small tornadoes, the Fosters' cabin still seemed small. I could see a reflection in the Fosters' window and knew that I was being watched through a pair of binoculars. Right then I had the chills and not just because I was cold. I lost a high school friend to a sniper's bullet in Vietnam. After that, whenever I felt I was being watched, I got nervous and always thought of Bobby. Terror is a hard thing; once you've experienced it there's no undoing it. You have to go forward and beat it. You can't go around it. You have to plow right through, or you'll never be worth anything. In war, you will die and maybe take others with you. When something triggers horrors from your past − even when you're safe on American soil, you have to deal with them all over again. You just do it. So I just kept plodding on, trying to think of something else. After another hour, I finally climbed over a three-foot snow bank on the lake's shore, only fifty feet from Chub and Fran's green ranch-style cabin.

Glad I was finally there, and freezing from my trek, I followed a snowmobile trail to the house, stepped onto the porch, and leaned my snowshoes against the inside wall. Chub, dressed in his robe, leaned on his walker to look out the living-room window. His hair was as white as the snow I'd been wading through. His face and arms were lineated and thin, almost frail. He continued watching me as Fran opened the door. Her hair was as white as Chub's, but much fuller and neatly combed. She was also well dressed. And while her face was lined, too, she was more rugged-looking than Chub.

Cracking the door about a foot, Fran stuck her head through. She looked at my coonskin hat and asked with a nervous twitch in her eyes, "Who are you? We've been watching you come across the lake."

"Yes, I knew you were watching," I said, after explaining who I was. "I saw the reflection of your binoculars in the window."

"Oh!" Fran put her hand over her mouth. "I'm really embarrassed. We just didn't know who you were. I'm sorry we didn't give you a better welcome. Please come in."

"Yup," Chub smiled, leaning forward on his walker and shaking my hand with a gorilla-like grip. "For a while there, you were going so slow, we thought you might be going backwards."

Chub didn't have any way of knowing how true his words rang. For a while I was going backwards, in time at least. But I brought myself out of it again. Every time I did, the past became more distant and easier to defeat.

"How did you know we were home?" Chub asked.

"I took a chance."

"Mighty long chance," he said. "It's three miles across that lake and another mile to where you had to park. It's durned cold out there, too."

"I thought it was about seventy degrees out. You mean it's colder than that?" I chuckled.

"If it ain't, you can walk on water," Chub said. "And if you can do that, you're welcome to stay as long as you want."

"I just walked on three miles of hard water, Chub. Does that mean I can stay?" Chub just looked at me and grinned.

Chub, 96, and Fran, 84, have histories that run as long and deep as Grand Lake Matagamon. Guides, game wardens, forest rangers, trappers—anybody who has anything to do with the woods—all visit the Fosters. In summer, people four-wheel drive six miles of dirt road. In winter, they ride snowmobiles, ski, snowshoe, or walk three miles across the lake to hear Chub and Fran's old stories, to check up on them, bring their mail, and give them a rundown on the latest outside news.

"I've got something for you," I said, after shaking the snow off my hat and boots and setting them on a mat in front of the door.

"Oh?" Fran asked, peering into the large trash bag I was opening. "What might that be?"

"Your mail. This is snowshoe mail delivery in the nineties, picked up after closing hours. I didn't come through

Patten until after eight last night."

"They let you have it! Wonderful! We haven't had any mail for a month now."

Fran's face was aglow, her voice excited, as she pawed through the mail and handed Chub a magazine. "They must have known Chub's medicine was in it. Thank you for carrying it all the way in."

While Fran was flipping through letter after letter, never opening any, just seeing whom they were from, Chub became engrossed in *Reminisce* magazine. When they get mail, these people are like kids at Christmas. While they opened the mail, I admired their cook stove. It was big enough to put four large cast-iron frying pans on the surface. Another stove, a gas cook stove, was built into the birch kitchen cabinets.

Walking over to the wood stove, Fran said, "If I gave up a stove, it wouldn't be this one." Throwing in a couple of sticks, she continued, "I bake all my biscuits, bread, and beans in this stove. We're pretty comfortable around here. You're leaning on a Maytag ringer washer. I used a scrub board for a long time. But now, nine hundred feet up that hill behind the house, we have a spring that gravity-feeds. It feeds both the upstairs and downstairs bathrooms and the kitchen."

The interior walls were all wood paneling. The ceilings were white tiles and the kitchen and bathroom floors were a glossy, inlaid tile. The living-room floor was covered with a red and black braided rug, the lights were gas, and a gas furnace supplemented their wood heat. Upstairs were five extra beds, all made up and ready for company. The same house on Moosehead Lake would cost over a hundred thousand dollars, plus. But Chub and Fran built it years ago when prices were much cheaper and they were making their living as guides. Chub was born Albert G. Gott in Bar Harbor in 1897. His father and mother separated around 1902, when he was about five. His mother went to work after that, and she worked until she died. Both Chub and his brother went to children's homes.

"The Fosters in Newry adopted me," Chub said, looking up from his magazine, when I asked how he got his name. "It was at Gould Academy in Bethel that I picked up my nickname from playing the part of a country boy named Chub in a school play."

Chub didn't have enough money to finish school at Gould. After only a year, he started doing odd jobs. In 1916, he joined the Army as a private in the cavalry, earning fifteen dollars a month.

Chub sipped on a glass of wine and rubbed his thumb against the fingertips of his right hand.

"They always paid us in silver dollars," Chub said. "I was down in Texas during the time of the Mexican bandit, Pancho Villa, but I never saw him. It was the same time Pershing, our general, was going after him. It always seemed to be a friendly thing. We used to go down to Rio Grande City, what they called Fort Ringo, across the river when the Mexicans had dances, and they always treated us good."

Chub sat in his chair, rambling on without embellishment. When I asked Chub if he ever added anything to his stories, Fran looked up from her mail and said with a smile, "He doesn't have to. He tells the same stories over and over to anyone who wants to listen. He knows them all by heart."

"Yup," Chub added with a little punch in his voice, "I tell them just exactly the way they happened."

In 1917, after the cavalry disbanded, Chub went to France during World War I.

"That wasn't such a friendly war," Chub said. "I was in four fronts as a mountain scout. They had horse artillery then."

"Here," Fran said, coming back from their bedroom. "Let me show you Chub's ribbon. It tells the different fronts he was in."

She handed the red ribbon to me, and I read:
AISNE – MARNE
ST. MIHIEL
MEUSE – ARGONNE
DEFENSIVE SECTOR

For eight months after the war, Chub stayed in Paris, until the private high school he was attending closed. "I missed the Maine woods, and those wonderful bean-hole beans," Chub said, smiling and rubbing his belly. "I swore if I ever got back to Maine, I was going to work at a lumber camp, just so I could have them good old baked beans. And that's just what I did."

Fran was born and raised in Patten. She first met Chub when he came into town with some folks who had hired him as a guide, but she didn't see him for a couple of years after that.

"Then one day he was back in town and we started seeing each other," Fran said.

"How did you like going out in the woods to live?" I asked.

"I didn't have much choice," Fran frowned. "But I really didn't mind."

Looking out the window at the late morning sun, she got up from the desk full of mail and headed into the kitchen, asking, "You'll have lunch with us, won't you?"

"Oh, yes!" Chub sat straight up in his seat. "You don't have to be in a hurry. You're welcome to have lunch. Stay for dinner, and seein's as how you can walk on water, you can spend the night, too. Stay as long as you want. We don't get many people to talk to."

"I can stay until tomorrow, so I can go to church on Sunday." I thanked them for the offer, and thought how hungry they must be for company.

Chub started working as a guide in 1920. He started out the same way most guides do today, working for different sporting camps and clubs. He also worked as a guide in Labrador, where Fran also worked as a cook. She showed me a photograph of freshly baked biscuits, bread, and donuts laid out on a picnic table beside a lake. She did all the cooking in a big tent.

"When we weren't in Labrador, Chub guided sportsmen that farmers took in," Fran said. "One of the last sporting camps he worked for was run by Virgil Lynch up near Ashland on the Machias River."

Chub chuckled at the mention of Virgil, saying, "I got to tell you about the Kellogg boys. Them boys were hellions. Their father was president of the American Tin Can Company. He sent them boys up to Virgil's with his chauffeur and I had to baby sit the rascals. I lost track of how many times they threw that poor chauffeur in the river," Chub said, laughing and moving his arms to illustrate. "One of those boys would grab the chauffeur's feet, the other his wrists, then they'd go to swinging and just let him fly. They were just having fun, so I never said anything. When they'd get tired of doing that, they'd get to fighting over some damn thing. And whatever it was they were fighting over always got thrown in the river. Time their folks picked them up, they near didn't have anything left, no camera, nothing. It was all in the bottom of the river."

In 1932, Chub and Fran were living in a log cabin at Lost Pond. Chub trapped beaver to earn a living. They didn't have many conveniences and still don't today. Fran said people today are spoiled.

"It's nice to have a few things," she said. "I kind of enjoy the running water that we have now. But I think most people, especially the younger generation, are pretty spoiled. If they had to live like I have over the years, they'd appreciate life a little more. While they're paying bills for all the wild doodads they think they've gotta have, Chub and I are enjoying this wild country." Fran looked out her kitchen window at the panoramic view, and said, "This is something you'd see on a postcard."

"Folks have it easy today," Chub said from his chair, leaning back for emphasis.

"It was a thirty-mile hike out of Lost Pond," Fran continued, following me from the kitchen to the living room. She poured Chub another glass of wine. "It took us two days anytime we snow shoed out of there. One time the snow was so deep, it took us seven hours to hike five miles. We stayed a lot of thirty-below winters there, before we opened the lodge."

"Yup," Chub tensed up, leaning forward in his chair. "One day when we were living there, I was off trapping beaver and fell through the ice with my snowshoes on."

"Yes," Fran said. "Not too long after that, they named the pond after Chub. It's been known as Snowshoe Pond ever since."

"Had a heck of a time getting out of the water onto hard ice," Chub continued. "Had to cut my snowshoes off to get out. Then I walked three miles in waist-deep snow, wearing frozen clothes, to get back to camp. I didn't have anything to make snowshoes with, so I took an axe and spent four or five days chopping a pair of skis out of a white ash tree. I used the skis until I killed a deer, then used his hide to make another pair of snowshoes."

Most guides would varnish up a story like that, I was thinking, but not Chub. Chub just went on talking; when he got carried away a little, Fran would point her finger at him, saying, "Now, Chub," just to keep him in line. Then he would add, grinning, "And that's just the way it happened."

In 1941, Chub and Fran started their own sporting camps — Fosters' Wilderness Camps on Grand Lake Matagamon. They stayed there for twenty-nine years.

Fran did the cooking and housekeeping at their camps and Chub did the guiding. They worked as a team all their life. "I always had hot meals ready and coffee on when Chub brought his guiding parties in from wherever," Fran continued, returning to the kitchen to check the potatoes.

"Yup," Chub added, standing up and leaning on his walker, "She always did it up mighty good. It was a two-mile trip across the lake to the landing where I picked up my parties. I'd either walk, skidoo, or boat. There were times when that lake would get plenty rough, and we'd be wet time we got back. I had an eighteen-foot aluminum boat with a thirty-five-horse Johnson's outboard that I picked folks up in. When we got back, food and coffee tasted some nice."

Chub had his own system for finding lost hunters. When a hunter got lost, he'd fire three shots. Then Chub would fire one shot in return. Then the hunter would answer with one return shot. Chub is proud of his record of always finding anyone from his parties who was lost.

"When a hunter gets lost," Chub said, sliding his walker into the kitchen so he could eat, "it's the guide who takes the heat. But I always pulled my own men out of the woods. Had a guy up here one time who spent a night out there. Ray Porter, the pilot who did all my flying for me, spotted the guy waist-deep in swamp water. The guy was out of his head. He swam across a stream. It took two men to chase and catch him. And it took him two days to completely straighten out. I don't know what happens to them. They just go crazy. And for what? There ain't nothing out there that's gonna eat them."

Chub was one of the last old-time guides. I've talked to several modern-day guides, and of those who knew Chub (and most did), they'd be the first to tell you that there were few men around who could use a setting-pole like Chub. A setting-pole is a wooden pole handmade from a small spruce tree, or store-bought with a metal tip. If a man knows how to use one, there isn't a much easier way to get up a stream. Chub would start from Matagamon, pole up Webster Stream, paddle Webster Lake, Telos Lake, Round Pond, and Chamberlain Lake, then pole up Allagash Stream to Allagash Lake with his parties. It's uphill all the way. He traveled the Allagash, Saint John, Penobscot, Aroostook, and Machias rivers, as well as streams and lakes and ponds too numerous to mention, either by snowshoe or canoe.

Chub and Fran gave up guiding in 1970 and sold their sporting camps the next year. Their camps are now a Boy Scout high-adventure base.

"I guided this other feller who thought his compass

always pointed toward camp," Chub said. "It didn't matter where your camp was, he thought his compass was supposed to point to it. I told him 'no.' He asked, 'Well, what's it good for then?' How can folks be that stupid? I don't hold it against them none, but I don't know what some of them are doing in the woods."

"Okay, boys," Fran said, crossing her eyes at Chub and putting dinner on the table. "It's time to eat. We can talk more later."

I slid my plate over and Fran filled it with ham, beets, string beans, and a large baked potato. We had our choice of water, milk, or juice, along with some of Fran's homemade bread. It was easy to understand why Chub and his parties enjoyed Fran's cooking.

Resettling in the living room after dinner, I was enjoying the wildlife paintings on the walls. One picture showed a guy chasing a deer with a rototiller. The tiller has handlebar steering, the throttle is stuck, and the man's feet are flying straight out, parallel to the ground. "Those were all painted by Jake Day," Chub said, letting go of his walker and sitting back in the recliner. "He's the artist who talked Walt Disney into using a white-tailed deer for Bambi."

"He did what?" I asked, surprised.

"Yup, ain't many folks know this," Chub said. "Old Jake worked at Disney for eight years. They were going to use a black-tailed deer. Jake told them that wasn't Bambi. Bambi had to be beautiful. So they sent Jake up here taking pictures for a year. He took pictures of everything: moss, lichen, flowers, trees, mountains, squirrels, everything. What he didn't take pictures of isn't worth talking about. He had a stack of pictures five feet tall when he went back. All the pictures for the movie 'Bambi' were taken right here." Chub pointed out the window to the surrounding mountains. "While he was taking pictures, the state of Maine sent two fawns out for Disney to monitor. That's how they created all the right movements in the animated Bambi."

"Well, isn't that something? I sure didn't know that."

"A lot of folks don't, but it happened just the same. Jake was good friends with Walt Disney and us. He was always showing Fran and me the pictures he took for Disney. You should see the picture of Pamola that Jake painted."

"A picture of who?" I asked, leaning forward in my chair.

"Pamola." Chub looked at me real serious. "You mean you never heard about Pamola?" Then he laughed, like he was incredulous. "He was the mythical Indian god of Mount Katahdin."

"Yes," Fran said, joining us after washing the dishes, "Jake was a good artist and friend. If you want to follow me down to the next camp, I'll show you the picture."

Looking back at Chub, she shook her head as we walked out the back door. "He sure likes to tell stories."

The painting showed Pamola with a moose head and antlers. He had a naked human upper torso with arms and hands. Eagle wings protruded from his back. His lower body was also human, but covered with eagle feathers to his knees, and he had feet and claws that looked like an eagle's. Pamola, who looked to be about twenty feet tall, was perched on top of Mount Katahdin, and Roy Dudley, the ranger who used to live there, was sitting in his hand. Roy was looking up at Pamola as they carried on a conversation.

"One of Roy's stories," Fran pointed to the picture, "has it that Pamola used to help the full moon get over Mount Katahdin. One night the moon hit the mountain and was stuck for three days. Pamola pushed and heaved until he finally loosened the moon and shoved it over the top. The moon went so fast that it rose and set three times that night trying to get back on schedule."

Chuckling, I asked Fran, "Who likes to tell more stories, you or Chub?"

With a wide grin, she stifled a laugh and turned and stepped out the door. On the way back, I took Fran's delicate but strong hand and helped her over the icy spots on the trail. She pointed out beechnuts and moose tracks, and even investigated the changing colors of the spruce tips. "Don't they smell wonderful?" she asked, holding one up for me.

As we walked across the backyard, Fran stopped. Pointing at the woodpile, she said, "We have a man cut our wood and haul it for us. Chub built a road in the mid-sixties." Then she looked up at me and whispered, "You know when we get low, I throw the wood in the shed when Chub isn't looking. He doesn't like me doing that."

In the woodshed that led to the house, Fran showed me the propane generator they use to run the TV, washing machine, and lights. The nearest public utility is seventeen miles away. "We have our phones, too," Fran said, opening the door into the house. "We had a friend call us on our radio phone all the way from France. It goes to a repeater and tower thirty-two miles away, out in Patten. Our crank phone is hooked to a cable that runs three miles under the lake to the dam. Three rings is for the dam; one ring is for us. We usually have about a two-dollar phone bill. We had a seven-dollar one once."

"Yup," Chub said, listening as we came in the door. "That was the phone we used when Fran had her quadruple heart bypass three years ago. She got all dressed up warm and then called the dam. They came and got her on a skidoo and took her across the lake. Then they took her by car to Houlton."

"They gave me this," Fran said, coming back from the bedroom with a baseball cap. "It says, 'I was bypassed in Bangor EMMC – Heart Team.' Neither one of us ever took medicine before that. We pay enough now."

"We're just beginning to learn what these old people have to go through," Chub added, pointing to the medicine bottle Fran was showing me.

Whenever they need medicine, groceries, mail, or other supplies, Fran jumps on their Yamaha Deluxe snowmobile and heads either up the road or across the lake; then she takes the car into Patten. But they usually buy enough groceries to last the winter before the road closes in with snow.

When they don't have company, Fran told me, Chub reads history books and books about Maine. He won't read novels.

Fran does some reading of her own, brings in the wood, and likes to go trout fishing. When they're not doing that, they sit and watch the chickadees and blue jays fly around with food in their mouths, and the nuthatches running up and down the trees backwards.

"We once had five tame foxes," she said. "I used to bathe them in the sink; then we'd all go for a walk or sit on the porch together."

"They were a sight to watch," Chub added, smiling at Fran, who had resumed reading her mail. "When I'd shoot at a squirrel and miss, those foxes would frown and frown bad. They expected me to get their meals for them. When I'd miss, they'd go chasing the squirrels off into the woods."

"We had a funny episode with a moose, too." Chub said.

He leaned forward, cupped his hands around his mouth and made a sound like, "A-OW, A-OW". "That's a moose call. We watched a moose swim across the lake once, so I kept calling him. First, I'd call him from the front of the house, then from the back. The moose was stamping his feet and running around the house trying to find the cow. Drool was running down his chin. Then he hooked his antlers into a tree. He got some ugly. I had to quit calling him—we thought he was going to break the windows!"

"That was quite a sight that day," Fran said. "But people talking about why we moved up here has been about as much fun as anything. And Chub, he just kind of adds fuel to the fire. People said we moved away from society, that we were hiding out from something, that I was living with a man much older than me, that Chub was Charlie Daniels and this was his retreat. One story was that we were nuts. We had a New Jersey woman up visiting once. She saw Chub take his gun out when the dog barked. She asked, 'Is the gun loaded?' Chub told her it was. So she asked, 'What if someone was out there stealing?' Chub said, 'I guess they'd be there come morning then, wouldn't they?'"

Then Fran got up, walked me to the porch door, pointed to Grand Lake Matagamon and the distant mountains, and said, "People don't know what they're missing not living here. The difference between us, and the people living in the everyday world is that Chub and I know both worlds, they only know theirs. Both are ways of life, but this is our way. It's not for everyone. But it's the way we like it. It's where we'll die."

Chub and Fran are both on the other side now looking down wondering if I'm ever going to publish this book. Chub probably still thinks I'm walking backwards.

•••••

(A deer crossing the road on the way to Oak Mountain Lodge.)

Chapter Eight
Monson
Oak Mountain Lodge

"Isn't that something," said the middle-aged woman ringing up my order at Monson General Store loud enough that even three old ladies bent over an ice cream cooler craned their necks to hear. "It sounds to me like you're in a pickle. You don't know where you're goin', how to get there, or who you're gonna see. Do you always hunt up folks livin' back in the woods you ain't even sure are existing?"

"It seems to be the best way of finding people," I said. "Generally, if there's anybody around living off the land, the locals know."

Wiping off the counter, she said, "Well, there is this one couple I know of, David and Janet Cormier. I can't tell you exactly where they live, but I do know they don't have electricity and they have to walk a ways into their place. You go up the road here and take your first right. Just keep asking directions as you go. Someone up that road will know where they live."

I drove about five miles up an old back country road and stopped for directions a few more times before the paved road ended and Festus started bouncing up a one-lane, winding dirt road. The first sign I came to said, "STOP." It was a regulation-red road sign spiked to a fir tree where everyone could see it. Behind it, to the left, a sign painted in black letters on a white board and nailed to a post on a wire gate read:

Charlie Reitze

PRIVATE ROAD
NO TURNS

(Oak Mountain Welcoming Signs.)

Most folks turn back when they see private road signs, especially two signs in the same place. I did give the matter some thought, but not much. I was curious to know how anyone was supposed to get back out of this country if they couldn't turn around. Neither sign said, "Trespassers Will Be Prostituted," as I once saw in Northern Maine.

A couple of miles farther, an old blue pickup sat parked in a grassy clearing at the base of a mountain where the road ended. I parked Festus and began hiking the footpath. The narrow footpath, about a half-mile long, was littered with brown leaves and pine needles as it snaked along, winding its way up the mountain under a dense canopy of hardwoods and conifers.

(Oak Mountain Lodge -- Footpath Stream Bridge.)

I worked my way through the trees, over a narrow footbridge, reentered the trees, crossed another wooden footbridge over a tiny stream and past a small pool, rocked up just big enough for someone to bathe. I continued up a steep, planked step-path that traversed a marshy area, then up another rise, until I finally saw a garrison-style home.

I walked carefully between the neat rows of the garden. The garden was terraced with four rows of well-placed trees where potatoes, carrots, onions, garlic, and bright blue and yellow columbines grew. Pole beans struggled to grow on a chicken-wire fence that was half flattened to the ground. The other half simply listed; fresh moose tracks revealed the reason. Dozens of three-foot-high stumps in the background attested to the work still required. Closer to the house there were two compost piles.

"Who is it?" I heard a voice ask from under the house.

Two dogs came bounding out, barking joyously. "Don't worry about the dogs," the voice continued. "They don't bite much, unless you're an assessor or from LURC or something."

Reaching out to pat the barking dogs, I spoke to them and tried to sound unafraid: "Calm down, I haven't eaten a dog since Vietnam."

I bent over and looked under the house, trying to see to whom I was speaking. "I'm working on a writing project about people and dogs living off the land," I said.

"Shut up!" the voice bellowed at the dogs before I had a chance to see the person underneath. Then the voice shouted to me, "Come around back. I'm piling wood under here for winter. The dogs won't bother you. They just like to bark."

That's good, I thought, just as one dog jumped up and tried to eat my face.

Around back, I was reassured when the voice's owner — a thin, bearded man dressed in light trousers and a checkered shirt — crawled out from under the house. He looked me over trying to determine if I posed a threat. Satisfied, he wiped his right hand off on his trousers and extended it. "Hi, I'm David Cormier. I figured you were an assessor or something. Usually no one else walks up the mountain."

"Is that why you have the posted signs down below?" I joked, hoping to put him at ease.

"No," he said, grinning, all hesitation gone from his voice. "They've been there for a long time. We just don't want anyone up here who disrespects nature. We live with the ecosystem. We won't have people destroying it. Let's go in the house." David brushed the dust off his pants. "Janet will want to talk with you. She must be busy, or she'd be out by now."

On the way into the house, David discussed his background. He was born and raised in Portsmouth, New Hampshire. At seventeen, he quit high school and started coming to Maine to visit his brother. By the time he reached eighteen, he was helping his father build a camp in Guilford. When the camp was finished, his father returned to New Hampshire, coming back to Maine only for vacations. David decided to stay. He lived alone at the camp for ten years, until he married Janet.

We walked to the kitchen table and he introduced me to Janet, who had just finished heating some herb tea. David offered me a chair at the table and poured three cups of tea. He then continued his story.

"I lived in the one-room cabin. I spent some of my time doing odd jobs, but mostly I backpacked. I hiked the Appalachian Trail and many other areas observing plants and wildlife. Being close to nature is one of the things I love the most. I did just what I felt like. And, of course, there was always tidying up around the camp to be done. Everyone around the Guilford area called me a hermit."

Janet chimed in, "Everybody talked about him. I kept hearing about this young hermit. Some of my friends knew David and were trying to get us together. He sounded really interesting. I wanted to meet him, and I knew his brother; it was him and some of my other friends who took me out in the woods to see David. But he was never home. He was always out hiking, so I left him notes to come visit me where I was living in Dover-Foxcroft."

"It was the neatness of his place that drew me to him," Janet continued, pushing ebony-black hair out of her eyes and sipping her tea. "It was as neat as a pin. You could tell by looking around that somebody who really cared lived there. I was impressed and just had to meet him. If he had been a slob, I wouldn't have gone back."

Janet grew up in the Pine Barrens of southern New Jersey. She lived in a cedar log home on a creek in the woods and heated the house with coal in potbelly stoves.

"I moved to Maine when I was 19 to attend UMO," she said. "After I got my degree in natural resource management, I got a job with the government and moved to Dover."

"In the summer, I lived in a teepee. In the winter, I lived in a tiny camp. You have to be neat to live like that. When David finally showed up, I was living in my teepee. We were both nervous," Janet said, laughing.

"Yeah," David agreed. "I kept coming home to those notes. So finally one day I decided to get it over with and I went to see her."

"We've been dating ever since," Janet added. "When people quit dating, their marriage tends to get dull."

"So, you see, we're both used to this naturalist way of life to some extent," David said, leaning back in his chair with a contented smile. "The quality of life here is A-1. It's great. We only have to work part-time.

"I'm a seasonal worker. We're both self-employed," David said, holding his callused, lineated hands out, palms up. "I plant black spruce and red pine for Champion Paper Company. Four of us planted eighteen hundred trees in a ten-hour day. We planted eighty to ninety thousand trees in three weeks. I also do blueberry harvesting in Cherryfield. Janet and I pick berries together, living out of the pickup. We always have money in the bank. We live on less than ten thousand a year.

Janet said, "It gives David and me a chance to earn some of our income together. When we're not working together, I work part-time as a soil scientist and do consulting for septic systems. While I'm doing that, David takes care of the chores around here. Right now, CMP is relicensing a dam on the outlet of the Kennebec. I have to determine whether any Indian artifacts found there are coming from natural soil or not."

"For the first time, we're where we really want to be," Janet continued. "We live right in the middle of an ecosystem. We study insects and various animals, and watch robins chasing Baltimore orioles. A toad comes to the house every day, and every day David takes it back to the garden. That's why we know we're made for each other. He'll do things like that and help protect the neighbor's land from erosion. He doesn't have to be asked. He just does it."

Janet glanced out the window at the dogs chasing a butterfly around the garden. The butterfly darted over a robin resting in the crotch of an old moose antler David had found and laid on a stump. Flying off, the robin landed on a nearby limb about ten feet off the ground. His head bobbed from one side to the other as he watched the dogs.

Janet got up and walked to the oven. She stuck a butter knife in a fresh loaf of bread. David, still sitting at the table, leaned his head back, inhaled the aroma, and said, "Honey, that sure smells good." Looking back at me, he asked, "Want some?"

Four words describe this couple and others like them: inventive, industrious, loving, devoted. If they can't find something to fit their needs, they make it. If they don't know how to make whatever it is they need, they buy a book and learn how. The Cormier home is a perfect example. David and Janet had never built a home without help. David learned some skills as a teenager helping his father build a camp, but this was a home. Here on the spur of a mountain in the north Maine woods, David and Janet built a home together. It was close to the finest, if not the finest, construction I had ever seen.

The Cormiers' self-employment afforded them time to hunt for the land they wanted and the time to build their house. The first time they saw this property, it was buried under four feet of snow, and they were on snowshoes. Even then they loved the sloped topography.

"We knew this was the place for us," David said, "when we first saw it. It isn't something we can put into words. It's just a feeling we had."

Locking eyes with me across the table, David said, "I guess if you're going to write about us, we'd rather you didn't give away our location."

After I agreed, David got up from the table and took me outside.

He showed me the teepee that he and Janet lived in during the summer and fall of 1989. Long, tapered poles leaned against the trees. The old canvas wrap was folded up on the ground.

"We lived in that until late October," he said. "We were always cold. I had a stove in the teepee until it caught on fire." David threw his hands straight up like flames bursting into the sky for emphasis. "We leaned a ladder against the teepee and ran up with buckets of water to put the fire out. After that, we used a fire pit. I wanted the house completely finished before we moved in, but the teepee got too cold for Janet. Before she came home from work one day, I moved everything into the house. We only had a curtain door, but at least she was warm, and we were happy."

Walking a short distance further, David pointed out the family shower. Grinning, he asked, "Do you want me to demonstrate it for you?"

"That's okay, not right now," I said, chuckling. The shower stall was triangular with a wooden floor and a roof held up by three sticks, with no closed-in walls. A black-plastic five-gallon jug sat on top of the shower, with a nozzle protruding down through the roof. When it was time for a shower, the Cormiers heated water on a nearby fireplace, poured it in the jug, stood underneath, and opened the nozzle. Now that was a real back-country shower.

(Oak Mountain Lodge -- Three-sided Bucket Shower.)

I asked what he would do if some stranger like me happened along while he was in the shower. David thought for a minute, and then chuckled and said, "No one ever comes by. Sometimes Janet bathes in the pool you saw coming up the trail. But it's way too cold for me to sit in. It's hard on the onions." David crossed his hands in front of his legs. "We'd have a better shower set up, but this is an unorganized township, regulated by LURC. This is all we're allowed. We lug our water and use an outhouse. Someday we're going to try and get a full system approved."

Hard and soft woods resembling a beaver motel were piled in front of the shower, waiting to be stored under the house or stacked nearby.

Neither David nor Janet believed in waste. If a tree died or fell, they used it. When they cleared their garden spot, they used every stick of every species for firewood or for building. They gathered the tiniest twigs of every tree for kindling. Anything that couldn't be used for kindling was used for mulch.

As David and I walked back out front, Janet stepped out of the house. "Let me show you the garden," she said, bending over to smell the columbines. "Then we'll have some pancakes. Everything is mixed and ready to go, but David likes to cook them."

The columbines came from the Swiss Alps. As a child, Janet visited Austria when her family lived in Germany for three years. A few years ago, she and David spent a couple of weeks visiting there. When they returned, they brought flowers with them.

As David went into the house to cook breakfast, she took me through the garden, pointing to the countless dead stumps that still needed to be pulled. "David and I felt that cutting and hacking the garden was a violent act. We pulled all the stumps in this part of the garden with shovels and a come-a-long. But you can't get too sensitive about cutting," Janet said as she walked over to the mulch piles, "or you wouldn't have a garden. It's okay if you do it without greed in mind and only use it for food and shelter. We don't use any commercial fertilizer, either."

"We build the garden as we have enough natural mulch to do it. That's what these two mulch piles are for. We don't strip a whole ecosystem to build a garden, like paper companies do when they cut trees," Janet explained as she pointed to the mountain ranges. "We live with nature. Every time David cuts, it's thought out. When he thins, he is healing the mess that was left from before. It's real personal to us. We're not living a movement, a one-time thing, like the hippie generation. We do this on our own."

"Yes," David said, joining us again. "It's natural. It's the way we live. It doesn't come out of a recipe book, and neither do the pancakes that I just finished cooking. Let's go in and eat."

The Cormiers spent about a thousand dollars a year on food. They bought eggs, cheese and milk at the closest store, which was several miles away. They purchased eight hundred pounds of bulk food like flour, rice, beans, lentils, split peas, macaroni, and bulgur[2] at a co-op in Dover-Foxcroft about thirty miles away. They lugged it all up the mountain in backpacks before the snow flies.

After breakfast, David pushed his plate aside and began talking about their house again. "We spent a month felling trees, a month hewing, and a month framing. What lumber we had to bring in, we lugged on our backs or pulled up on skis in the snow. I wanted to do it just like it was done in the

---

[2] wheat that has been partially cooked, cracked, and dried

old days."

David pointed out the window at the footpath going down the mountain, "The house sits on railroad ties that we pushed and pulled up that trail, one by one, on a ski nailed to the bottom of them. What we didn't bring up on the snow, we lugged a little at a time." Pointing at the Glenwood cook stove, David said, "That stove, and the airtight Waterford in the new addition, we hauled in pieces on skis, with a pry bar behind to push them."

"And all this land around the garden and the house," David turned his hands palms up, showing me the calluses, "was cleared with a broadax, chainsaw, and come-a-long. I didn't use the chainsaw for building the house. I only used it to help clear the land. We had to compromise that much. But the original part of the house is all done the old way."

"You know what makes this place?" Janet asked, sitting back at the table. Before I could say anything, she put her arm around David, and grinned. "There're no roads. We can't hear cars. We have to snowshoe a mile up the road, then a quarter-mile up the mountain to get here."

Every time I looked at them, they were either grinning, smiling, or winking at each other. If they weren't doing that, they were holding hands. They shared the same ideals in land and in love, they cooked together, and they worked on the house and in the garden together. They're friends, they're lovers, they're a team.

Their house was made of hand-hewn, dovetailed, self-locking timbers that David patiently worked from round wood. He used a crosscut saw to fell the trees, a broadax to shape the timbers, a drawknife to make the round pegs that lock the timbers together, and a hand drill to make the holes. They brought in rough-sawn hemlock boards for the siding, roofing, and sub-flooring. Old motor oil was used for a preservative on the siding, and they had a metal roof. They have a solar panel to run the fluorescent lights, and use kerosene and candle backups for long winter days. Their phone is a remote FM system that signals from the antenna to a receiver at a neighbor's deer farm down the mountain. The new addition is twenty by twenty-four feet.

"We need more room," David said, still sitting at the table, and pointing through the door into the new part. "I heard of this idea of using a chainsaw to rip slabs off a tree to make timbers. That's what I did. One beam is six by eight inches. I didn't want to take as long to build this new part, so I used a chainsaw, and we bought more material. We have three-and-a-half-inch insulation in all our walls. I made the windows and the wall covering is cloth fabric that we got from Guilford Industries."

"People don't think this kind of life is possible," Janet added, getting up and pouring us another cup of mint tea. "Society thinks when you're not working it has a negative effect. Well, we are working. We're just not working for a wage. We work for ourselves. A lot of people would see this as poverty. Not us. We love it."

I asked myself what is poverty, if not relative? Is poverty having two nine-to-five jobs, five days a week, with all the overtime you can get to make the payments on your expensive house, two cars, snowmobile, and boat, not to mention all the insurance payments, and electric bills? Or is poverty living on less than ten thousand a year, building and owning your home on the side of a mountain, stepping out your back door to snowshoe, ski, hike or bike whenever you want, and visiting Alaska and Austria.

"We call this Eichenberg-hütte," Janet said, looking at

David, "because our home and topography are a lot like where we stayed in Austria. They live in small huts there. We live in a small place here. They hike from hut to hut. While we were there, we hiked from hut to hut. Their animals are up in the high country. Our animals here are up in the high country. 'Eichen' means oak, 'berg' means mountain, and of course, 'hütte' means hut. So we live in our Eichenberg-hütte, or Oak Mountain Lodge."

(The Cormiers and Oak Mountain Lodge)

"This is a life," David added, as we all went outside so I could take some photographs before leaving, heading in some other unknown direction. A few minutes later, as I turned toward the trail, David picked up the moose antler that the robin had been sitting on. Looking me in the eye as he handed it to me, he said, "It's sacred to us."

"Our place here is an end. It's where we'll spend our

life," David concluded.

Knowing what David meant, how he and Janet felt, I rested the antler over my shoulder. Looking at them with their original cabin in the background, I thought for a minute about the others I had met. The way they live and their love for nature were similar. It seemed that they were from the same mold–and bound by a common thread. I shook their outstretched hands, thanking them, then turned and pensively walked down the mountain. Slowly, Eichenberg-hütte disappeared from view. Once again, I was alone.

Janet died from cancer a few years later. Her ashes are spread on the mountain.

(Russell Mountain.)

(Oak Mountain Lodge Compost Garden.)

(Oak Mountain Lodge Showing New and Original Home.)

Chapter Nine
Chesuncook Lake
The Lost Village

Chesuncook Village rests peacefully on the northern end of Chesuncook Lake's western shore, just across from Gero Island. Chesuncook once was a town of farmers, loggers and trappers; a place where weekends were spent gulping hooch and dancing backwoods jigs. Today, it's a village of hunting and fishing cabins where tourists go to take secluded vacations and canoeists stop for a good meal and to rest after long paddles across the lake.

I found myself there because my brother Ray, a registered Maine Guide and teacher of outdoor survival, told me that Chesuncook was the only place he knew of in inland Maine that you can only reach by boat or plane. Only four people lived in the village. Bert and Maggie McBurnie ran the Chesuncook House, the oldest place in the village. A short distance up the lake, Jack Downing ran a smaller, newer lodge. And Jack Murphy, up the lake still a little further, built and repaired rifle stocks.

"The man's an artist when it comes to wood," Ray said. "He sells homemade root beer, too, and fresh bread, donuts, and cookies. He will even make you supper. He throws roast beef, potatoes, and vegetables all in the same pot on a wood stove. It was a helluva meal we had."

My mouth was watering so much when my brother finished describing the meal that I knew I had to visit Chesuncook – if for no other reason than just to have dinner.

It was four a.m. on a hot July day a week later, when I left for Chesuncook with Owen Stinson, a fishing buddy and fellow church member from Wilton. It was good to have Owen along. I knew the conversation would be clean and he'd be a great support to me, even if he didn't realize it.

Owen was excited about seeing the far-off lakes and villages and meeting some of the people I'd been telling him about. It would take us four hours to drive from my house in Canaan to the Chesuncook Dam, then another five hours to paddle the eighteen miles up Chesuncook Lake to the village, located northeast of Moosehead Lake in Piscataquis County. Thoreau visited Chesuncook on his famous trip through Maine in the mid-1800s.

"We won't get home before midnight," I told Owen, passing him a calorie-free chocolate donut. About five miles north of the unorganized territory of Kokadjo, I stopped Festus so Owen could lean out the window and snap a picture of a small bull moose ambling across the dirt logging road.

By eight a.m., we were loading our gear into my eighteen-foot cedar-strip canoe. I had hoped for a calm day, but by nine we had three-foot whitecaps rolling out of the north, splashing Owen in the bow. Every time a wave hit him, I'd lean back in my seat, thinking I'm glad it's not me up there, and roar with laughter. Owen would turn around, tug his hat down to his eyebrows, and give me a disgusted look that made me think he questioned my sanity.

By ten, Owen needed to dry out, warm up, and put on his rain gear, so I put ashore. Sitting on a driftwood log, Owen wiggled his toes in the white sand, looked straight up into the sky, and said, "That sun really feels good." But I only half heard him.

I was back in Vietnam on three days of R&R wiggling my toes in the sands of the South China Sea, thinking about the chopper ride to get back to my base and fighting that ugly, bloody war. Owen sensed I was someplace else. He waved his hands in front of my face and asked, "Where you been?"

"Oh, back in another world," I commented, shaking my head. I really didn't want to talk about it so I said we might as well get going. Paddling off the shore I thought, "This isn't Vietnam. It isn't the South China Sea. And I don't have to go back to fighting a war, so why do I have to keep thinking about it?" I was mad at myself.

In the next three hours, we had to go ashore twice more to empty water out of the canoe. All the while, Owen mumbled, "I'd like to get you up here just once. You keep laughing and you might get wet anyway."

As we paddled the final stretch to Chesuncook Village, I just chuckled and said, "That's okay, on the way back you can take the stern." Knowing Owen couldn't get at me, I rubbed it in some: "A little water don't bother me none."

I was thinking about a book I had been reading, and feeling much like the teacher who went to Chesuncook Village in 1932. In her book, *Chesuncook Memories*, Lana Nottage Gagnon says, "Finally, after eighteen or twenty miles of water, water everywhere, and seemingly numberless hours, in the distance, I saw Chesuncook . . . with neat, trim buildings nestling on the shore."

Finally, I guided the canoe into a rocky cove on the shores of Chesuncook Village. Owen jumped out, dragged the canoe up on shore and snapped it sideways, trying to dump me; he would have succeeded if I hadn't anticipated his move and braced myself with the paddle. We walked up the path and collapsed on the McBurnie's front lawn.

After resting a few minutes to eat a couple of peanut-butter sandwiches, Owen asked, "Wanna go see who the six-foot hulk is nailing on that overgrown float up beside the barn?"

"I just got comfortable," I groaned. "You mean I gotta move?"

"Yup," Owen said, "if you wanna get anything done. Don't get him mad at ya. I bet he dresses off around two-seventy or -eighty pounds." Owen went to look at the garden and I walked up to the float to introduce myself.

"Hi," was the only reply, as he continued nailing.

My immediate thought was, "This guy doesn't want to talk to anyone foolish enough to paddle the length of Chesuncook in a wooden canoe, carrying only a notebook and a camera." But when I flooded him with questions like, "Are you Bert McBurnie? Where did the name *Suncook* come from? How long have you lived here? Do you grow most of the food in the garden?" he seemed to have a change of heart. He tossed his hammer across the float to a rusty coffee can full of nails, then sat down with his chin in the palm of his hand and his elbow resting on his knee, as if to say, "If I don't answer this guy's questions, I'll never get anything done."

"Yup, I'm Bert McBurnie," he said. "You must have seen the name *Suncook* on one of the cabins coming up the lake."

"Yup, I did, or rather my friend, Owen – he's over there admiring your garden – did. We were curious; how come *Suncook* and not *Chesuncook*?"

"Well, I'll tell ya," Bert said, increasingly friendly as he pushed a couple of nails away from the edge of the float. "The natives have always called the village Suncook to differentiate it from Chesuncook Lake. They call themselves

'Suncookers.' As for when this village got started, well, beats the hell outta me. I don't know when the first cabin was built, but there was one here in 1845 when Thoreau came through."

"I do know," Bert continued, cuffing a honeybee off his knee and pointing across the lake to Mount Katahdin, "I'd rather be a Suncooker than a stressed-out pressure cooker living a tense city life. I like Thoreau's philosophy: If you don't need it, chuck it. There's always plenty to do without anything extra. If I'm not guidin', I'm workin' on the house or one of the cabins. If I'm not doin' that, I'm gettin' in wood or workin' in the garden. But what's nice is, I don't have someone pushing me to meet a deadline.

"I'll tell ya, though," Bert said, grinning, "ya gotta like this kind of life. Nothin' here comes easy and everything else comes hard."

(Bert McBurnie hauling supplies.)

Bert pointed out over the lake. "See that red and white plane comin' in over where your friend's walkin'? Well, they're some friends that I've got to go shuffle down the lake to one of my cabins. Why don't you get your buddy and walk around and look the place over? Maggie's up to the house. I'll be busy for a while." Bert jumped on his four-wheel ATV and headed over to the plane taxiing up to the old dock.

Owen was engrossed in watching the plane, so I left him and walked toward the house. Purple lilacs and pink mallow flowers grew in bunches around the house; white mallow flowers skirted the lawn. A woman who could only be Maggie stepped off the front porch to meet me. The lineaments of time that marked Maggie's face and her torpid eyes reminded me of Katherine Hepburn in *Rooster Cogburn*. She was dressed comfortably in a short-sleeved, light-blue blouse, tan trousers, and a brimmed straw hat.

Putting on dark sunglasses and pointing to the flowers, her first words to me were, "Those mallow flowers belong to the geranium family." She spoke slowly, in what sounded like a drawn-out French brogue. "They were planted by the side of the house when it was originally built back in the eighteen hundreds. They're a tough flower to have lasted all these years. They grow bushy, like lilacs and, as you can see, they're as tall as the eaves of the house.

"The bees love them. In the evening," Maggie said, cupping her hands up to her chest, "the blossoms close around the bees, giving them a cozy warm home for the night."

She pulled a branch closer, smelling the flowers, then pushed another fragrant branch toward me. "You don't hear much about them anymore; they're an old-fashioned flower."

Maggie was so friendly that she didn't need to ask who I was or seem to care that I was taping our one-sided conversation. She had seen me talking to Bert and knew he would never let me by if he didn't approve.

"Let me tell you about our home," Maggie continued, inviting me to sit on the porch. "This was always known as the Chesuncook House. It was first built as an eighty-foot log structure in 1849. In 1863, the present-day Chesuncook House was built. Of course, it was a lot more secluded back then. It's still quite remote, but we have a two-way radio to Greenville."

(Chesuncook Lake House.)

Maggie's eyes brightened, her voice pitched a little higher. "We have a cellular phone now, too. I don't know if you noticed, but Bert's hooked up solar panels on the roof. We have all the modern conveniences, from bright lights and heat to hot water. But I still cook on the woodstove, and that's the way I like it."

Maggie waved to Bert as he passed by on the four-wheeler, pulling a loaded wagon down to a cabin on the

(Chesuncook Lake with Mount Katahdin in the background.)

edge of the lake. She continued, "Bert guides hunters and fishermen. We can accommodate twelve to nineteen people, between the house and the lakeside cabins. Not everyone comes in by plane. Quite often, Bert makes the eighteen-mile trip down the lake in his boat – it's a twenty-foot Starcraft – and picks people up at the old Chesuncook Dam."

Waving to the four people who were walking along the edge of the lake, Maggie called out an invitation for coffee after they were settled. She then started in on another subject. "If our guests stay in the cabins, they have to cook their meals and keep their fires going. That costs them twenty dollars a day. If they stay here at the house, we offer them what we call The American Plan, for seventy-eight dollars a day. That includes meals and heat. If people call ahead, they can have fresh lobster or anything else. Bert just goes down to Greenville and gets whatever they want."

Maggie made it sound like a ten-minute stroll to Greenville, located at the southern end of Moosehead Lake. But it must take at least half a day. Still, they had done it so many times that it had become part of their lives.

Suddenly standing, Maggie said politely but matter-of-factly, "I've talked long enough, and haven't given you a chance to say much. But we can talk more later. It's time for me to be doing my chores, the grass is getting tall up at the cemetery."

She grabbed the lawnmower parked beside the porch, pushed it across the lawn up a small path and disappeared into the woods. I knew I hadn't said anything wrong because I hadn't said anything at all. So I just figured she had chores, like Bert, who was still relaying guests' supplies from the plane to their cabin.

I found Owen sprawled on the lawn between a couple of beautiful white birch trees, his hands folded behind his head. The remains of a peanut-butter sandwich protruded from his mouth, moving back and forth and gradually disappearing into his face. He looked like a rabbit chewing grass.

The McBurnie's green lawn was like a huge, lush golf course. Even the grass growing close to the trees was mowed. The birch trees were tall and robust — the most beautiful I had ever seen. The rippling, crystalline water of the lake sparkled like blue sapphires against the dark and light green forests, with a stunning backdrop of Mount Katahdin.

After I ate a couple of sandwiches, we began a self-guided tour of the village. Not far from the birch trees, and just above the dock where the plane was moored, was a small white building about the size of two outhouses. A sign painted in bright-red block letters read:

CHESUNCOOK VILLAGE
VOLUNTEER FIRE DEPT.
ENGINE 1 PUMP 15

Looking inside, we could see a manual water pump (or Indian pump), a modern gas-powered water pump, shovels, rakes, and other fire-fighting tools. In the distance were several well kept log and clapboard-sided camps and homes, a white vinyl-sided church, and Jack Downing's lodge. Owen watched a black duck swim around the shore of the lake while I snapped photos of the brown wooden sign in front of the lodge. The sign read:

KATAHDIN VIEW LODGE & CAMPS
GUIDING, BOAT RENTAL, BOAT
TAXI, T-SHIRTS & LODGING

Up a short pathway from the Katahdin View Lodge was Jack Murphy's, the only store in the village. He wasn't there, so we didn't have an opportunity to enjoy his cooking.

We walked over to the church. A sign on the front of the church porch read:

CHESUNCOOK VILLAGE CHURCH

While it didn't look like the church I attended, it was sweet and quaint and had a good spirit about it. It felt good to be setting my life in order and going to church every week. Seeing the church brought tears of joy to my eyes. Owen could see that it affected me, but chose not to say anything.

The small church sits comfortably back from the shore on a grassy knoll. Towering boreal spruce and fir rise to the north, their outstretched limbs reaching for the sky, dwarfing the steeple. To the east, Mount Katahdin's distant, rugged peaks take on a blue hue that blends with the water of Chesuncook Lake. Two small, white-clapboard cabins sit off to the south side, for parsonages. And to the west is a meadow the size of a football field, bordered by dense forest and small camps.

Scattered throughout the woods surrounding the church, we saw tarpaper cabins, cedar-shingle cabins, clapboarded cabins, and a few log cabins. Owen decided which one he wanted. Standing on the porch, he said, "This is about as close as I'll ever get to owning it."

A footpath behind the church wound through the fir trees and up another knoll, back through the woods to the cemetery where Maggie was mowing. The gravestones leaned slightly, rising about a foot above the carpet of grass.

Many were inscribed with the name Smith and dated back to the eighteen hundreds. One stone read simply, "Peter Tomah," there was no date. Seeing us at that gravestone, Maggie shut off the mower, walked over and told us, "He was an Indian, one of the first settlers of the village."

(Chesuncook Lake Cemetery -- Maggie McBurnie.)

After I introduced Owen, he asked Maggie, "How long have you and Bert lived here?"

Wiping the sweat from her forehead, Maggie answered, "Gosh, I married Bert in Paris when he was in the military. He moved to the village with his parents in 1935, when he was four, from Aroostook County. He's lived here ever since, except for six years in the military during the Korean War. I moved here in fifty-six. I go back to Paris every couple of years, you know. But I'm always awful glad to come home. When I first saw this place, I fell in love with it. You can't begin to imagine how wonderful it is until you live here."

Chewing on a piece of grass, Maggie continued, "There's always plenty to do. I keep the grass mowed, work in the garden, and do most of the cooking. Bert does all the heavy work. All the supplies and lumber we need he hauls in on the boat. But we still have some supplies that we either forget or can't plan for, and they have to be brought in by snowmobile. It's easier now than it used to be. Back in the old days, they hauled everything in on horses, wagons, or sleds. Those trips couldn't be made in a day, so folks camped out along the way."

After talking for several more minutes, Owen turned to me and said, "I hear Bert back there nailing on the float. While you talk to him, I'm gonna see what's on TV in that outhouse with the antenna on it. I can't think of a better place for a TV."

Maggie reached down to pull the starter rope on the mower. "I'll never get this mowed if I don't get going. I'll see you boys back at the house."

Walking back to Bert, I asked him if he had another hammer. "No," he said, "go ahead and ask away. I didn't want to do this now anyway." When I asked if they used the church, Bert put his hammer down and sat on the float, "You bet we do. Starting in July, I go down the lake once a week and bring up a new preacher to preach to us savages. Ministers come from all over the country. We get a new one every week and they get a vacation. That's the way it's always been around here. You never know how many Suncookers are going to be here. The preachers just preach to who ever happens to be here."

Bert nodded in the direction of the church and continued, "The church used to be the old village school. We

149

converted it a few years back. I went to school there for seven years – well, until there weren't enough students left up here to keep it open."

"You know, back around 1880 or 1890, the locals had their own postage stamps," Bert said, starting in on another subject. He stood up and stretched his back, then sat back down and continued, "They were called the Tourist Dispatch, Chesuncook Locals, and Maine Moose stamps; they were sold by locals to defray the cost of delivering mail to the remote hunting and fishing camps. Now I boat eighteen miles, three times a week, to the old Chesuncook Dam for the mail."

"How did this village happen to be built so far away from anything?"

"It didn't just happen," Bert said, waving his arms in a wide arc. "If you stop and think about it, most towns are about twelve to fifteen miles apart. Look at Bangor to Orono, Newport to Pittsfield, Greenville to Lily Bay, Lily Bay to Kokadjo, Kokadjo to Grant Farm, Grant Farm to Morris Farm, Morris Farm to Chesuncook Dam, and the dam to here. These towns and others around the state are as far apart as oxen could travel in a day. Most people don't know their history."

"What did they do up here back in the eighteen hundreds?"

"Everybody was making a fortune. From about 1820 to 1840, they sold ship masts for three hundred dollars a piece. They cut the masts out of huge virgin pine trees." Bert stretched his arms out as far as they'd go, saying, "Three men couldn't wrap their arms around one of those trees. The Englishmen came up here in the seventeen hundreds and carved big arrows in the trees. That was their mark and nobody else could cut them – they were for the King's ships, and the king paid dearly for them." With a nail, Bert carved a big arrow in the float and said, "They looked like this. They also traded shiploads of lumber for shiploads of rum. There were more than two hundred and fifty people in the village back then, and I think they drank more rum per capita than anywhere else in the world. You should talk to Oscar Gagnon. He stays out at Chesuncook Dam or down to Greenville. His wife Lana was my schoolteacher. He can tell you a lot of stories about this place."

"What a way to live," Owen said, just then joining us.

"Yeah, we like it," Bert answered, smiling.

"I checked out your outhouse, but I didn't stay long. You took out the TV."

"Yeah, folks were spending too much time in there," Bert joked. "Listen, I ain't trying to rush you boys, but if you're gonna get off this lake before it gets too late, you better be on your way. Come back anytime you're a mind to, but stop and see Oscar; he can tell you anything you want to know." As quick as that, Bert left us to go meet Maggie, who was coming back from the cemetery.

"You mind if I take the stern?" Owen asked, as we walked to the canoe.

"Nope," I said. "Have at it. I'll lie down and rest my back."

The wind was in our favor, but picked up soon after we got on the water. It came up so fast and hard that it made me nervous. We were in the middle of the lake, and I knew better. I got up and grabbed my paddle just as a wave picked the stern up right out of the water. We were breaching four- to six-foot swells. Every time we crested, I could see daylight under the bow or the stern. Driving my paddle deep, I had to make some hellacious draws to keep us from going broadside. Owen looked worried, and I knew just how he felt. We fought the waves for an hour and forty minutes. When we hit shore, I was one happy camper. Owen didn't say anything, but I knew he was, too. We had made the trip back in less than half the time it had taken us to get there.

On the way home Owen spoke about how lucky we were to get off that lake safe. He said, "I was praying all the way. I thought we were goners."

"I was praying, too," I said. "I know better than to get out in the middle of that lake, especially in a canoe.

•••••

After that first trip to Chesuncook, I went to Greenville three times before I caught up with Oscar Gagnon in October. Once I got him started, the history and stories poured out. Sitting back in his living-room recliner, sipping a cup of coffee, Oscar said, "The Indians named Chesuncook. They called it the Great Goose Meeting Place because of all the geese stopping on their way south."

"I moved there in 1926, when I was twelve. Chesuncook was quite a town back then. It was an organized town with three selectmen, a tax collector, a schoolteacher, a teacher's assistant, a road commissioner, and a deputy sheriff. People moved to Chesuncook during The Depression to farm. My great-uncle was a priest; he moved there and had cows and horses like everyone else. They all ended up liking it and most of them made forestry their way of life. Some, like myself, trapped."

"The town went back to the state because of debt, though," Oscar chuckled. "The families running the town borrowed money from the state's till. They couldn't pay the debt, so the Great Northern Paper Company did, with the understanding that the town would go back to the state. You see, now the Great Northern will deny this, but everyone knows they didn't want us there anyway, especially as an organized town. This was its chance to force the town back into wild land. No one went to jail over it, because the bill got paid. Now the folks living there have to pay a wild land tax."

"When was the church built?"

Scratching his head, Oscar said, "That church was built by the Great Northern in 1922 out on Gero Island. It was originally built as a school. In 1926, it was moved off the island. They hauled it across the ice with a Fordson tractor to where it is now. In 1974, we repaired it and converted it to a church using my late wife Lana's book money."

Oscar paused, his eyes suddenly misty.

"Gero Island used to be all fields, ya know. Actually, it wasn't an island until they put the bigger dam in, so they could back up more water and ship more wood. But it's an island now and it's eight miles around it. They used to grow hay, potatoes, turnips, carrots, and beets, and keep horses on the island. The Great Northern bought most of what they grew. What it didn't buy was sold to the lumber camps. We called them 'horse-tote camps' because the only way you could get to them was on horses. The teamsters hauled everything to the camps with horses and wagons. They'd be out on the island pitching hay on the wagons, then hauling it off to the camps. Those wagons would be rounded right over." Oscar gestured with his arms. "It wasn't all woods behind the village back then either; there was over three hundred acres of garden. It's all grown up now."

With a little prodding, I learned that the islanders

gambled for entertainment and made their own hooch for the festivities. The brew was made with corn and wheat, and fermented with yeast. "It was quite potent," Oscar said. According to local legend and Oscar, it ended when representatives from the Great Northern got the Geros drunk one night and tricked them into signing over the island. Great Northern always vehemently denied such accusations. In any event, after the paper company took possession, things changed. According to Oscar, the Geros had to leave and the Great Northern pastured from seventy-five to a hundred horses on the island. More than fifty horses at a time were loaded on a scow down at the old Chesuncook Dam and transported the eighteen miles to Gero Island. The horses not on the island hauled logs back in the woods.

"Did you go up and see the cemetery?" Oscar asked, as he stood up and stretched.

"Yes, I talked with Maggie up there while she mowed the grass."

"That cemetery used to be down by the waterfront. We moved it before they put in the bigger dam. I can tell ya a few stories about that." Oscar said, then put his feet up on a hassock and cackled like an old ghost. "It used to be called Graveyard Point. Somebody out hunting accidentally got shot. Tom Anderson, one of the early settlers, said they had to shoot the guy to start the cemetery." He chuckled and pointed to a picture of the cemetery hanging on the living-room wall.

"When we dug up the graves to move the cemetery, some of the skeletons were on their faces. You see, back then some people were buried alive. The doctors pronounced them dead. Everyone thought they were dead, but they really wasn't. They'd wake up in their casket and try to claw their way out. That's why they have embalming now," Oscar said, squirming in his seat. "We found where a squirrel had dug down into one of the graves and built a nest in somebody's skull. Charlie Smith, an old trapper who knew the guy, said he always had nuts in his head anyway."

In the spring, the trappers gathered at the hotel for the wardens to stamp their beaver pelts.

"The wardens and us trappers used to have a big time of it, and some got mighty drunk. I never did, though," Oscar said, grinning. "Mrs. Eddy (the woman who ran the old hotel) hated drinking and she'd get awful mad."

"It sounds like making hooch was quite a thing back then."

"I still don't have to go very far to get it," Oscar said, chuckling. "Reckon we better go eat now. We've got moose meat, vegetables, and baked taters, if you're hungry."

As we ate our dinner, three deer – a doe and two fawns – ate theirs in Oscar's garden, right under the kitchen window. We watched them for several minutes before they disappeared into the dense forest behind the house.

After dinner, Oscar settled in his chair and began another story.

"Once I get started telling stories, I hate to stop," he said. "I want to make a tape of some of the things that went on over the years, so people can listen to it after I die. I don't dare to now. Some of those folks are still alive and I'd have a price on my head!"

Leaning back in the recliner, Oscar told of two brothers who were in the hooch business. "These two brothers, Bob and Bill Farrell, squatted and built a camp next to the lake on Great Northern land. The Great Northern had a big passenger ship – a crude-oil burner propelled by a paddle wheel, just like the old Mississippi riverboats. One day they hooked it up to the Farrells' camp and towed it out into the lake. After that, the brothers built a big scow and lived on it. It was run by a one-lunger gas engine. The boys named the boat *The Temple of Knowledge*. All they did was make and sell hooch for a living," Oscar chuckled, licking his lips. "The wardens couldn't catch them – their stills were in different spots around the lake – and they were somewhere different every day."

"When I was young," Oscar continued, pointing to the rack of antlers hanging on his knotty-pine wall, "come winter, we'd see anywhere from thirty to forty caribou out on the lake at a time. Those antlers are more than a hundred years old. The caribou were a pretty sight, until a sawfly epidemic killed all the low-growth juniper that they fed on in the winter. They ate the moss that grew on it. Within two years after the junipers were gone, the caribou were gone, too. You can't make the biologists understand that,"

Oscar continued, looking exasperated. "Like a lot of folks, they think hunting pressure drove them out. It didn't, no more than it's driving out the deer. I lived in the woods. I know what drove the caribou out, and I've told the biologists, but they're too smart to listen."

"I spent a lot of good years at Chesuncook," Oscar said. "I left after Lana passed away. She's buried down here. It was good livin'. I still spend my summers at Chesuncook Dam."

Oscar summed it up best when I was stepping out the door to leave. He said, "You know, old Charlie Smith was part Indian. I asked him one time if he ever got lost. 'Lost,' he said. 'I got lost when I was a kid. I liked it so much here that I stayed lost.'"

I went back to Chesuncook the summer of 2016. Nothing had changed much - just the owners. In March 2018, the main Chesuncook House burned down. It is being rebuilt.

(Jim Quinnam Bird Hunting.)

(Jim Quinnam Riding his Horse on an Atlantic Ocean Beach.)

Chapter Ten
Waldoboro
The Mysterious Stranger

Searching for people when you don't have names is always a challenge. Locating Jim Quinnam proved even more difficult, more fun, and more unsettling than most.

As usual, I left home one July day with no idea where I was going. I only knew that I wanted to interview a fisherman. Winding along country roads from Augusta to the coast, I enjoyed a breathtaking view of rolling hills woven with a tapestry of red, blue, white, and golden flowers. Then I was suddenly assaulted by an arresting odor – a skunk? I knew better. It reminded me of my days working on a dairy farm.

Around the next corner stood a small roadside store. The sign on the roof read: *Russell's Store, Cowshit Corner, Newcastle, Maine.* Across the road, Mr. Russell told me, were "287 Holsteins, eatin', mooin', and shittin'."

Interesting, yes. But my goal was to find a fisherman, so I went looking for help.

In Damariscotta, the postmaster couldn't (or wouldn't) help me. I was too disgusted to ask an obese woman who was busy picking her nose at the roadside fish stand. Three lobstermen couldn't think of anyone. A Penobscot Indian informed me indignantly that he wasn't a tour guide. A code enforcement officer, wearing a ten-gallon hat with a six-shooter strapped to his hip, seemed too important to ask. An arrogant state cop snarled, "Can't you see I'm busy?"

I finally weaseled Jim Quinnam's name out of the owner of the Rising Tide Health Food Store after spending an hour installing shelves in a cooler. However, I'm not really sure who weaseled what out of whom.

"He lives somewhere in Waldoboro," she said, ringing up the orange juice that I thought she might have given me for my time. "I have no idea where. His mailing address is Wiscasset, if that helps."

"Wiscasset's thirty miles from Waldoboro," I said. Thinking about a guy who lived that far from his mailing address sent shivers up my spine. I knew he didn't want to be found. "Do you know what he does for work?"

"All I know is that he used to fish. Now he lives in the woods and shoes horses."

"Well, that's something," I said, paying for the juice. Heading out the door, I was happy the search had taken a new twist. Now I had a name at least, and began thinking of ways to break the ice when I met Jim.

I also continued to look for help.

Two gangly teenagers pumping gas at the Texaco station in Waldoboro said they didn't know anything. The cashier was more knowledgeable. Scratching her chin, she said, "I don't know him, but check at Genther's Store up the road. If they can't help you, come back and I'll call a friend. She might know Mr. Quinnam."

The owner of Genther's had never heard of Jim but, as luck would have it, the ragged-looking, bearded customer standing at the counter had. When I said Jim's name, he spun around like a soldier executing an about-face.

"Why do you want to see him?" he demanded.

"I'm working on a book about people living off the land," I said.

After looking me up and down, he seemed satisfied and gave me directions to Jim Quinnam's or at least to his general location.

I moved on.

"I'm looking for Jim Quinnam," I said to a man working under the hood of a car.

"Well, he don't live here."

"I know. He lives up back. You know if he's home?"

"Nope. Might be, though." He cocked his head around, looked up at me from under the hood, and scowled. "Saw his girlfriend go in a few hours ago. Ain't seen her come back out. He's got more girlfriends than a dog's got fleas. Never know which one's in there, nor how many."

I started into the woods.

The huge junkyard hidden behind the trees beyond the house didn't surprise me nearly as much as the crater-size mud holes and the graveyard of rocks in the road around the next bend. Alders slapped at both sides of my truck like giant octopuses. Swamp water, a foot deep, hid the rock that stopped Festus short, bending the stabilizer arm and freezing the steering. Mosquitoes, dense trees, and murky water conjured up memories of firefights in Vietnam.

Any time I drove down a muddy road, especially a road with dense bushes slapping at the side of my truck, unwanted memories of monsoon rains, foot-deep mud roads, rice paddies, and fire fights still haunted me. On this day, it wasn't so bad; it's just that it was there. And it was still there on occasion, despite all the progress I had made in the past couple of years, especially of late. It was often enough to wonder if the past would ever be the past. I doubted it, not entirely, at least.

Tears welled up again, wetting my cheeks. I wished I

could go home, I mean, home to where I used to be, home to the carefree years before Vietnam. But that was a fantasy. Always, there would be another road, another rifle going off somewhere in the distance, another explosion from some construction field, or another road with alders slapping my truck. Always, there would be something that would trigger another memory – and I hated it. And so I continued to learn the best ways to force my thoughts back to the present. This day, the most pressing concern was Festus. After maneuvering Festus off the rock, I realized I would have to remove the stabilizer arm to steer – not an easy task. Since I only brought two sets of clothes for a weeklong trip, and since I was totally alone, I stripped and worked naked in the muddy water. Resting my head on a rock, I glanced toward my feet and laughed uproariously. With only my big toes protruding above water, I looked like a double-headed turtle, and felt quite silly. But, it took my mind off Vietnam and kept my clothes dry.

(Festus.)

After about a half hour, I dried off with an old chamois cloth. By that time, I was wondering if I'd ever get to Jim's and even if I still wanted to. The road didn't look any better ahead. Nonetheless, I put Festus in gear and spun and dug and bounced through the mud holes. I tried to stay between the alders until the road ended.

The walk in proved as interesting as the drive. I headed up the swamp-grass wagon road with my camera slung over my shoulder. Halfway in, I noticed a fifty-pound bag of lime on the side of the road. I had my icebreaker.

After a mile walk, with ten toes parboiled in ooze from the mucky road and hordes of insects attacking me with stingers as big as baseball bats, I broke through the woods into a clearing that was Jim's front yard. The late afternoon sun warmed me as I stepped into the clearing. Off to my right, across the combination yard/pasture, a horse was nosing around the corner of a small red barn. To my left, in a copse of white birches, a small vegetable garden flourished. Two chained-up bird dogs yapped at me worse than my ex. In front of me was a huge A-frame house with no exposed walls. The roof looked like it grew right out of the ground.

But it was an ugly black collie bolting across the yard, growling like a she-bear protecting her cubs that really caught my attention. Teeth bared, he slid to a stop five feet away. One hand was ready to drop the bag of lime on the dog and the other held my Canon protectively below my waist. Imitating Crocodile Dundee, I stared that canine down. He growled. I growled. He growled again. I tried to spit in his eye like John Wayne did to a dog on one of his movies. I missed, and then hollered, "Get outta here, dog, before I rip your face off."

He wasn't impressed.

Inhaling deeply, I turned sideways to face him, edged bravely past him and gradually backed my way to the front door. Stalking and growling, he was ready to pounce the instant I lost eye contact — which I was not about to let happen.

Feeling the raised hackles on my neck, I knocked on the door, hoping that Jim was home. The arched door, swung slowly open on squeaky, quarter-inch steel strap-hinges. Standing before me, clad only in a white towel, was a huge man – short in stature, only about five-foot-six – but massively built. The expression on his face wasn't exactly welcoming.

Oh wicked, I thought, he doesn't wear clothes and he's going to sic that dog on me. I pulled the camera closer.

"Who are you?" he demanded.

My gut feeling was that he thought I was a cop. I had to sell myself, and I had to do it quickly. "I'm a writer," I answered, which didn't ease the tension at all. Thankfully, his next questions did.

"How did you find me, and what are you doing with that bag of lime?"

Answering, the first question would have taken too long; the second proved to be my icebreaker, which was my intent.

"Well," I answered, "it was beside a puddle on the road. You must have lost it when you were hauling it in. I figured you'd do the same for me. You would, wouldn't you?"

I knew the question would put him on the defensive.

"Well, yeah," he stammered, caught off guard. I knew then I had won the ball game.

"Put that bag down. You don't have to stand there holding it all day," he said, more subdued. "Come on in. I just don't believe it – I have to know how you got here." He scratched his head and sat down at the kitchen table.

"I give people directions and they still can't find me," he said. "And then here you come walking right up to my front door, right past that ugly dog and carrying fifty pounds of lime."

His round and beady dark brown eyes stared at me from across the square oak table. Not moving, not blinking, just staring – a blank stare, like someone spaced-out on dope. But he wasn't spaced-out. He was alert — feeling for the truth as I spent the better part of the next hour explaining how I located him.

When I finished, he said, "Probably more people know about me than I'm aware of. I still don't know who the hell down there would tell you how to get here. But I'm unusual enough that word gets around. Listen, it's gettin' kinda late. You wanna sleep in the hayloft? We can talk more in the mornin'."

"If you don't mind," I said.

"Want a sleeping bag?"

"No, I'll get mine from the truck. But you'll have to grab that collie."

In the barn, lying comfortably on newly baled hay, I fell asleep to the sound of horses stomping and munching and the sweet aroma of fresh-cut clover. I awoke the next morning to dogs barking, chickens clucking, and roosters crowing while Jim fed them. He hollered, "You up, Charlie?"

"Yes. I've been lying here listening to your critters. It reminds me of the farm where I grew up."

"Breakfast is on. Havin' oatmeal, if you want some."

"You bet. I'll be right down."

"If you need the outhouse, it's on the hill just beyond the barn. Toilet paper's on the hub of a wagon wheel leanin' against the wall. By the way, I hope you get along with hornets! There's a nest in the roof."

Walking through the mucky barnyard up a hill, I was reluctant to use the outhouse. Inside, two hornets buzzed around a nest making me more nervous. I was careful not to make any sudden movements, and was relieved when I stepped back outside.

Jim was pouring hot oatmeal in a bowl as I pulled a chair up to the table. "Yellow jackets didn't bother you none?" he asked.

"Nope. You would have heard me if they had. You ever give any thought to moving that nest? It's bigger than a football."

"No, that's their home. They're part of the farm. I've been here fifteen years, and they've been here almost as long. I think they followed me up from Wiscasset, where I grew up. Me and them hornets, we're like Edward Abbey; we like living in the outback. You ever read any of his books?" Jim asked, sipping a glass of milk.

"Yes, I have. *The Journey Home* is my favorite," I replied, stirring honey into my cereal. "I can see where you'd like him."

"One of my girlfriends reads passages to me," Jim said, reaching down to pat the collie, who minded everything Jim said. "He worked for the park service somewhere in Arizona and tourists would always ask him the same question: 'When you gonna pave this road?' Mr. Abbey would answer. 'The day I leave.'"

Jim went on, "If people complained about the drive in here, he'd probably say, 'If you don't like it, get outta the car and walk. Take that bra off and brown up those old white tits.'" He laughed.

"I used to have to tow my car with the horses, until I hauled in some gravel with that old dump truck down by the bridge. The road wasn't in good shape when I first got here. Now it's as good as it needs to be. If people want me, they can walk like you did. There's something insulting about a truck goin' by your front door. It disrupts your privacy. When I first moved here, I had a fella come in on a four-wheeler when I was out ridin' my horse. He asked two questions. He didn't get no answers. I put that horse's head down and headed right at him."

"Good oatmeal," I said, eating the last of it. I pulled a book off the shelf beside the table.

"Yeah, I add cinnamon. It gives it a kick. That's a good book you've got there: *European Civilization*. I read a lot," Jim said, picking up another. "*The Rise of the American Colonization* – I like this one the best. I've got a lot of books upstairs that I got when I was in college. I have a degree in sociology from U. Maine in Portland."

"Do you use your degree?" I asked, returning the book to the shelf.

"Every time I make a decision," Jim said, pouring another glass of milk. "Right now, I'm reading a book about the origin of the English language, how we misuse some of the words. Because of the out-of-state influence, my own language is getting a bit adulterated. I noticed yours is some, too."

"How so?" I asked.

"A few minutes ago, you said, 'These ones.' Using 'ones' behind 'these' is redundant."

"That's true," I said, smiling. "And besides that, you don't need it."

Jim grinned and pulled his degree out of another book to show me. "I don't use my degree as much as I could. I don't need much money to live. I cut my firewood with a bucksaw. Sometimes I use an old chainsaw, but not often. The bucksaw keeps things peaceful. I grow and cut my hay, and most of my food, too. My philosophy is, just don't let money change hands any more than it has to. Mostly, I shoe horses." Jim set his spoon on the table and turned his callused hands palms up. "I'm a farrier. I also do underwater photography and some weddings, too. I shuttle the bride and groom to their reception in my black carriage. It looks good with my two whites, Tonka and Browser. I have a chestnut too – Skeeter – but I don't use him for weddings."

Jim cleared the dishes off the table and put them in the sink. "Do you know how to ride?"

"Yes. I had a horse all during junior high and high school."

"Wanna ride down to the river after I finish here?"

"That would be fun," I said. "I haven't ridden a horse in a long time. I'd like to go for a swim and get cleaned up anyway. You mind if I look around a bit?" I asked, getting up from the table. "I've been admiring your kitchen door," I said, walking over to it. "I've never seen one four inches thick. And the rounded-arch design kind of goes with your A-frame, especially where you have the exposed beams."

"I can't take all the credit for building that door," Jim said, drying the last of the dishes. "A friend helped me build the house. Three of my girlfriends helped, too. They're all from the other world, the real world. One of them worked at a boatyard – that's how I got my rafters and part of the doorframe. This side of the door has a piece of historical wood in it; it's planking off the *Bowdoin*. It sailed out of Wiscasset to the North Pole with Admiral Peary. I horsed everything in on a wagon, sleigh, or pung." A pung is a sleigh with a boxlike body. Jim made one out of an old pickup.

(Jim Quinnam in front of his home.)

"What do you think of those skylights?" Jim asked, pointing up to the dining-room ceiling. "They're portholes out of different ships. I got them up to Elmer's Barn in Coopers Mills. He runs a big antique business. Different parts of the house come from all over. Some of the wood and glass has historical value. Part of the oak finish in the living room is colonial trim from Senator Margaret Chase Smith's father's home."

"Those rafters must have been fun to put up," I said, looking up at the twenty-foot peak.

"They had to be put up in pairs. I pulled them up with a

block-and-tackle and a team of horses. That's what makes this home; it has a variety to it, not just where I got my materials, but the ways I built it," Jim spoke with obvious pride as he put the dishes away in pine cabinets. "The kitchen floor and countertop are inch-and-a-quarter slate that I got from the hippie fair. Each piece weighs four hundred pounds. I had five pieces and four women – two on the front of the wagon, two on the back."

"You keep up with four women?" I asked, while running my hand over the smoothness of the countertop.

"No, but it looks good, you know. I used to keep three around all the time. If one got mad, I could live with the other two. Now I got one who won't tolerate it. She has to put up with me, and she says that's enough. When I had three, we always had fun. They were havin' fun the day I hauled in the slate, till the bridge broke and the horses went right over the side. The wagon stayed on the bridge, but it stove up the harnesses, so I sent a couple of the girls to get a yoke. When I got it hooked back up, the wagon fell off, and I lost all the slate down in the brook. Had to twitch it out."

"You don't have anything in here lightweight, do you? What kind of walls are these?" I asked, looking at the dining room.

"*Zintax*, with white stucco. Two of those sticks weigh about four pounds. They're over four inches thick, you know, good insulation. I'm quite comfortable. This is a Fisher wood stove." Jim stepped back from the sink and put a frying pan on the stove. "It keeps this place plenty warm. The chimney's an eight-inch steel CMP underground water pipe; the copper tubing wrapped around the top heats most of my water. I have gas backup."

The rest of Jim's house is pine board walls and floors.

The bathroom is sheet rocked, painted white, with a porthole window in the wall behind the claw foot tub. A gold-colored, sheathed sword leans against the wall beside the tub. There is no phone in the house, but he has a two-way radio. The lights run off solar power.

We had talked so long in the house that Jim finally offered me some woodchuck and beet greens for a snack before we went riding.

As we saddled the horses, Jim never took his eyes off me. He wasn't sure if I could ride like I said or, if being from the "other world," was a city boy who couldn't drive anything more than an automatic. It wasn't until I mounted and neck-reined my horse that I could see Jim was confident. Outside the barn, his few chickens sounded like a thousand when we passed by, and his hound dogs barked like they had treed a coon.

"Calm down, Mingo," Jim hollered to the black-haired dog. "You too, Latico," he yelled at the off-white. "We ain't goin' huntin'. Every time I get the horses out, they start barking. They love to hunt. I shoot birds off of Skeet's back," Jim said, looking back over his shoulder as we entered the woods. "I taught one dog to wear sunglasses, smoke a pipe, and walk up and down a ladder."

"When I first moved here," Jim said, moving to the side of the trail so I could come up beside him, "I dressed up on Halloween as a desperado. I was wearing a Marlboro Man jacket and cowboy hat, and I took my horse to a bar in Bath that used to be a church. I rode right up to the bar, pulled my coat back to expose my gun, and said, 'Give me a sarsaparilla.' The lady bartender said, 'We'd like you to leave your horse outside.' I said, 'You must be Miss Kitty. You'll have to wait till I finish this drink.' Someone else asked,

'What the hell are you doin' in here with that horse?' I asked, 'What the hell you doin' in here afoot?' I shot my gun blanks outside, then went to the American Legion Hall and did the same thing. After that, I got outta Dodge." (When we returned to the house later, Jim showed me a newspaper clipping with a heading that read, "Mysterious Horseman Rides into Bar.")

It was a half-mile to the stream from where we tethered the horses. Jim went for a walk to give me some privacy. I stripped and jumped in, feeling a little self-conscious. Laughing to myself at his story, I wondered if he was telling tall tales. He was crazy enough to be telling the truth.

After we returned to the house, Jim dismounted behind the barn. "Listen," he said. "I have to get a load of hay. You wanna come?"

"No, thanks," I replied. "I need to be heading up into The County."

"Suit yourself," Jim said. He handed me a brush and started to brush his sweating horse down. "I'll give you a ride out in the back of my wagon."

Hooking the same two horses up to the wagon, Jim attached the neck yoke to the top of the driving saddle. He was using light driving harnesses instead of draft harnesses. I couldn't see how he had any control over the pole between the horses – it was a real jillpoke outfit. But I had complete confidence in him – he seemed to know exactly what he was doing.

I rode, or actually bounced, out in the back of the wagon. Jim sat on a single-board seat resting on each side of the wagon. He said, "Every time a man makes a decision, he draws on past experience. When I moved here, it was because of negative experiences I had in towns, like my father had before me. Dad got in trouble once for pissing where someone could see him. Here I can bathe in the river, then walk naked to the outhouse, work in the garden, or run in the field."

(Jim Quinnam Harnessing Up.)

Stopping the wagon behind my truck, Jim said, "You take it easy. Come back any time." He snapped the reins and continued, "A guy I know who was pretty tired of the rat race once said to me, 'Years ago, men worked like hell to get away from the old ways. Now we work like hell to get back to them.' I guess I'm back."

My son Jared and I visited with Jim not too long ago. He hasn't changed any, and neither has his dog.

•••••

(Jim Quinnam.)

Chapter Eleven
Chain of Ponds
Generations

Many times I have returned to the Chain of Ponds and Dead River in Eustis, Maine. There, like E.B. White described in "Once More by the Lake," I have sought the "placidity" of old haunts where I enjoyed so many good times as a child. I would grab my fishing pole and head off to Snow Mountain Pond, my favorite fishing spot many years ago. Like soup in a bowl, this pond is cupped in a basin with the surrounding mountains casting their reflection on the pond's quiet surface. Perched on ledges that jut out into the pond is an old forest rangers' log cabin.

(Charlie Reitze feeding Gorby Birds at Snow Mountain Pond.)

Evenings I stood on the porch with breadcrumbs in the

palm of my out-stretched hand, inviting the Canadian Jays to alight and feed. The sharp pointed nails of their tiny feet pricked the skin of my fingers as they alit and pecked the morsels from my palms. After feeding for a time, they would fill their beaks with breadcrumbs, fly off, store the crumbs, and return for more. Often I sat on that old porch feeding the Jays, and had quite a good time doing it. It's one of those things that a man always remembers.

Only a few feet from the porch is a clear, cold, bubbling spring – always a welcome treat after the three-mile hike up the mountain. Green, towering fir, spruce, and pine trees grow in the surrounding area, which is also filled with a deep, soft, cool moss. After feeding the jays, I used to walk peacefully through the maze of rabbit and deer trails, roll in the velvety moss, skinny dip in the cool waters of the pond, then lay on the moss and soak up the sunshine.

E.B. White took his young son to another favorite lake. "On the journey over to the lake," he wrote, "I began to wonder what it would be like. I wondered how time would have marred this unique, this holy spot – the coves and streams, the hills that the sun set behind. The camps and the paths behind the camps."

Thinking of White, I took my eight-year-old son, Shane, to my Dad's old camp in Eustis. For the first time since my childhood, I became excited at the prospect of seeing the old camp, and wondered how it would look. Would it still have multi-colored shingles on the roof? Would there be electricity now? Would the driveway still be two wheel-ruts snaking through the spruce and fir? How much had the new owners changed it?

The camp was basically the same as I remembered it — the old driveway, the roof shingles, the piney aroma, and the lack of electricity. However, a bottled gas tank had replaced the woodpile and through a window, I could see that a hot air furnace had replaced the old wood stove. The changes saddened me. No longer could you cook crisp black toast on the wood stove. Gazing at the camp, the old outhouse, and the trails I had blazed through the forest so long ago, I hoped I could give Shane some pleasant memories, too.

(Chain of Ponds as Seen From Scenic Overlook.)

I stood with my son as Dad once did with me, on the same worn out dam that separated the Chain of Ponds from the Dead River. Here my son caught his first trout, just as I once had. I cast the fly and as soon as I hooked a trout, I passed the pole to Shane and helped him reel in the fish. Shane held the pole while I controlled the line – his face aglow with excitement, his laughter full of joy. It was then I realized, as White once had, "that the years were a mirage and there had been no years." I felt like a young boy again, reliving my life. Shane was I, and I was Shane.

The water cascaded over the dam like it always had. Leaves floated and bobbed on the rippled surface of the small eddy in the river. The clear water revealed the rocks covering the floor of the outlet. Trout darted through the pristine water, shadowing the rocks beneath them as they passed. I looked at the boy who was silently watching the red and white Doodle Bug fly as it trailed his floating line. It was my hands that seemingly held his fly pole, my eyes watching his. Tears welled up and filled my eyes. I knew that all too soon my son would grow, become a man, and like I had, move on.

We caught six trout that day. Shane helped me cook them on the banks of the Chain of Ponds. I built a small rock fireplace and placed the fry pan on the hot coals after my tepee fire had burned down. It was only a couple of minutes before the trout sizzled to a golden brown. Looking up at the clear blue sky, and feeling the intense heat from the baking sun, I thought, "What a beautiful day to be here with my son." As the trout were frying, I reached down and picked up my boy; weeping, I hugged and kissed him. I knew that in time he too would cross this same path, and only then would he understand my tears.

Shane and I fished and camped for a few days. I spent the time teaching Shane how to fly fish. He, unknowingly, spent his time healing me. It was good to see his smile, to hear his laugh. It put me at peace. Often over the years, when alone, I would weep. Vietnam was always there. When Shane was with me, Vietnam was not. It was a short few days that we were together on this trip, but it was a time of healing. I tried to see life through Shane's eyes. And as I looked at life through the eyes of a boy, I was at peace for a short time, but in that short time I was able to rest from the horrors of war.

(Natanis Point Campground as Seen from Chain of Ponds Overlook.)

Shane caught the first and only fish on our last day. He cleaned it. He cooked it. We ate it. After we ate, he looked up at me, and in his boyish wisdom, said, "Dad, sometimes you look sad. But today you are happy. Gram said, 'Sometimes your father is thinking about Vietnam.'"

"Yes, son," I said, "sometimes I do feel sad, but being with you makes me happy. Maybe when you're older we will talk about Vietnam." Picking Shane up, I hugged him again, and said, "It's time to go, son." So we packed up. I took Shane home, went to church the next Sunday, and then headed north for another interview.

Chapter Twelve
Linneus
It's Home

A long-faced, middle-aged woman, standing taller than six feet and wearing black loose-fitting trousers with no shoes, leaned on her Blazer. She was pumping gas at the convenience store in the town of Linneus, just south of Houlton.

An old potato farmer putted down Main Street on a John Deere tractor, holding onto his straw hat as three logging trucks jostled by.

"Nice day," I said, looking up at the woman as I filled Festus at the next pump over.

"Every day we get up is a nice day," she chuckled. "Say, that's a fine-looking canoe you have there. Going fishing?"

"No. I'm working on a book about people living off the land. I have to paddle into some places. You wouldn't happen to know where Jere and Ley Armen live, would you?"

"Well, I know you won't have to paddle to get to them, but you can't drive either, unless you have four-wheel drive," she answered, putting the nozzle back on the gas pump, and looking real close at my canoe. "Cedar strip, isn't it? You make it?"

"Yes, to both questions," I replied.

"It's absolutely beautiful. You did a wonderful job. Ley would love to see this. He appreciates good work. I'm Jere

Armen." She reached out to shake my hand.

"Say what!" I exclaimed. "I don't believe this! What a coincidence."

"Oh, this is no coincidence. Things always happen for a reason," she said. "I don't know why, but we were supposed to meet. Let's discuss it back at the house. The kids are waiting for breakfast. When you're ready, go back to the red house on top of the hill. My driveway runs along the left side of the house. You can only drive in about a quarter-mile, that's about halfway. I'll see you when you get there."

Sandwiched between acres of dogwood bushes, the Armen's grassy, two-wheel-rut driveway looked more like a tractor road. Where I parked, the road disappeared into a huge mud hole, reemerged several feet later, only to disappear into another mud hole. The wheel ruts were almost deep enough to engulf my truck, so I walked the rest of the way, skirting mud holes and jumping from grassy hummock to grassy hummock.

The dogwood bushes ended where the Armen's dooryard began, at the edge of an old potato field where unfenced sheep ran helter-skelter. Cats and chickens shared the muddy yard and the rundown, open sheep pen. It looked like a turn-of-the-century farm.

The muddy Blazer was parked in front of what I first took to be a ramshackle part tar-papered, and part log barn. The roof bellied, like an old mixing bowl. The place looked sadly un-kept and ancient. Then, I realized that it might actually be their home. "It can't be," I thought. "It looks like it belongs in a ghost town."

The house had been built in two sections with a foot-wide alley separating them. The only thing that connected the roofs was a sheet of tin flashing. The roof shingles were curled and flaking off the older section and those on the new section weren't much better. There didn't appear to be any foundation. The bottom logs were rotting into the ground and the upper logs were dark, punky, and collapsing around those under them.

As I walked closer and stood beside the garden, I still was not sure if the building was a barn, an old horse hobble, or a house. The question was answered when Jere Armen stepped out of the entryway. Her hands were resting on the shoulders of her young son. Her teenaged daughter, who was standing behind her peeking over her shoulder, was wearing blue cutoffs. Her hair was almost as long as her mom's. Framed by the doorway, the trio looked wonderfully happy and content despite living under such humble circumstances. Jere's hands rested reassuringly on the boy's shoulders as her daughter whispered something to her. Jere turned her head and nodded. I sensed a powerful, almost mystical spirit between mother, daughter, and son. But there was something more. There was an unmistakable bond of love. It wasn't something you could see. It was just there. It was so natural – nothing false about it. Its richness permeated the air, giving me a joyous feeling. I was reminded that it isn't *where* you live that matters, but *how*.

Standing by the garden, looking at mother, son, and daughter, I was too far away to speak without yelling, so I didn't say anything. The silence was sacred.

The garden was at peak growth, heavy with produce. Green tomatoes were giving way to ripe, red ones and pepper plants bent over and touched the ground. Shoulder-high corn stretched, reaching for the sun. Potatoes, green and lush, grew from well-manicured hills. Onions, cucumbers, beans, and peas grew in perfect rows, with not a plant out of place, or a weed to encumber growth.

"Are these your children?" I asked, reaching the front door.

"Yes, this is Moira, my first, she's sixteen," Jere said. "And this is my baby, Ramon." He shied away, hugging his mother's knees. "He's six. I have two more. My second, Krystl, is off at a horse camp today. And Todd, my third, is in a program for talented youth at Hampshire College in Amherst, Massachusetts. He's twelve."

Changing the subject, Moira pointed toward the garden and spoke for the first time. "Mom, is there a reason for that tomato plant to be all droopy?"

"Wow, you're really observant," I said, looking at Moira as we all walked toward the garden.

"You get that way living close to the earth," Jere said. "It goes with the territory. There's something rich about the soil oozing up between our toes. That's why we don't wear shoes. We know the soil, it's part of us. More to the point, we're part of it. We've been here for eighteen years. This land is part of our family now and we're extremely conscious of how we use it."

"I like your philosophy," I said, bending down to inspect the drooping plant with Jere and Moira. "You live what you preach."

"When we first got here," Jere continued, "this soil was terribly poor. It took a while to build it up, but we did it by using the animal waste. We have thirty-five sheep, several chickens, and more rabbits than I can count. When the kids were little, we had a couple of goats for milk. Later we traded them for a cow. Now we buy our milk but we still have our own eggs, wool, and lamb chops, and we have a horse for pulling wood. We have two hundred acres for firewood, and we built our home from that wood. Down back, there's a sawmill that Ley built. We even milled our own logs. I'll have him show it to you after we go to the house. He's busy writing on his computer now."

Following Jere, I said, "You must spend endless hours canning."

"I guess I do," she answered, gently placing her arms around the kids' shoulders. "But everyone has a job. It's all done as a family. We put up more than a hundred quarts of pickles, several quarts of blueberry, raspberry, strawberry, and chokecherry jam, and about ten gallons of applesauce. We can everything you see in the garden. It all goes in the root cellar with our bulk foods."

"We can peas too," Ramon added.

"Oh yes, that's right, I forgot," she said, as we stepped into the kitchen.

The clutter in the kitchen appalled me. Old cardboard and newspapers were stuffed in ceiling cracks for insulation and pieces hung down like confetti, ready to fall. The woodstove was rusted, full of pockmarks, and ready to collapse. Under the woodstove, tinder-dry woodchips and bark were scattered, mixed with more newspaper and cardboard. It was a death trap waiting to explode in flames.

With arms folded, Jere leaned against the old woodstove. "That's a lovely stove over there beside the refrigerator," she said. "It has eight burners, three ovens, and a warming oven. When we could afford LP gas, it was really a labor of love cooking Thanksgiving dinner on it. But since we haven't had the money for gas, we use it to set things on. We use the refrigerator for storage. I pump cold water from the well and put it in the 'fridge for milk and other stuff we want to keep cold. By changing the water a couple of times a day, it stays around forty-five or fifty degrees."

(Jere Armen, "It's home.")

Behind the stove and refrigerator, five shelves loaded with canned goods and other supplies covered the entire wall. Several five-gallon buckets of food were set on the floor under the first shelf. Other buckets were scattered around the kitchen. There was no wall, no nook, no cranny that wasn't stacked with food and supplies. The only open area was a narrow walkway. In the middle of the room, the floor humped up a foot from an old stump that was forcing its way in as the house settled. The floor tapered off in all directions.

Sensing the presence of another person in the room, I turned, and there, framed by the entry to the original section of the house, stood a man who could only be Ley. He wore faded jeans that were baggy enough for two people. He was as thin as Olive Oyl. His dark, scraggly hair hung down to his shoulders. He had powerful, penetrating eyes. I walked over to shake his hand, wondering how cordial he would be considering that he hadn't ventured outside to introduce himself. Not knowing what else to say, I said, "Your wife tells me you have a computer. Without electricity, how do you run it?"

"I have a generator," he answered, standing motionless. Suddenly, his face brightened and his eyes widened. The change in his demeanor occurred so fast that it surprised me.

"Come here, I'll show you my office," he said, disappearing through the three-foot-wide opening that couldn't have been more than four-and-a-half-feet high. I had to bend over to prevent my head from hitting logs that had been hacked out with a chainsaw.

"Man, this is wall-to-wall books in here!" I said. I sat down at an old school desk in front of a bookshelf. "You must do a great deal of writing. That old Macintosh works off a generator?"

"Yes. It works good. The power surges don't seem to bother it," Ley said, sitting in front of his computer and looking back at me. "I'm writing a novel about the city of Atlantis now. This is my third book. The other ones were titled *The Peace Tax Fund* and *Conscientious Objection to Military Taxation*. I'm a pacifist, so half of my tax dollars going to military buildup doesn't square with my conscience. When I wrote about the IRS, it was amazing — they came crawling out of the woodwork. I mean it was almost like Communist Russia.

"It was a lifelong dream we both had to come here, to leave Massachusetts and get away from all that kind of government domination. Working in the smog and traffic and hubbub was a real downer. This is a life of voluntary simplicity — we're living our vision. Now all I do is pick blueberries, plant trees, and write. Jere teaches at the high school part-time and clerks at a lawyer's office up in Houlton. Here, we can live in today's society, yet not compromise our ideals. And while we're living in the wilderness, we are not running away to the wilderness. That would be like running away from our ideals, not sharing them. We're convinced that we're more than three-dimensional people. And it's that spirit that guides our lives – we like to share with society."

"We've known each other since we were kids," Jere said, coming in from the other room and sitting down beside Ley. "I knew his folks, and was visiting them one day when he returned from Northeastern University. After that we just kind of grew together. Ley harmonizes with the land. He doesn't have the consumer frame of mind, and he's a man of power. I connected with that."

"I never did get to finish my education," Ley said, changing the subject while thumbing through a book. "It was interrupted by the draft."

Out the window I could see Moira and Ramon working in the garden. Moira was hoeing dirt up against the potatoes while Ramon, using a sprinkler can, dumped water on the pepper plants. Watching the kids, I wondered what Jere meant by "a man of power." Ley had changed the subject so abruptly that I knew he didn't want to discuss it.

"I was more fortunate," Jere continued. "I got to finish mine. I graduated magna cum laude from Tufts University with a BA degree. I spent my junior year at the University of Tubingen in Germany. Ley joined me after finishing his alternate service as a conscientious objector at Children's Hospital in Boston. We lived in a garden house. Ley wrote music and poetry. It was like living here in a lot of ways. There was no electricity, no water, but it gave us ideas. We almost took up squatters' rights on a section of terrace land there, but decided owning our own land would be better, so we came here. There was encouragement in the fact that a lot of people were giving up their comfortable existence to come here. Back then there was a lot of spiritual support. And our families supported us. His father bought us the Foxfire books, and then my father bought us a cream separator. They have always helped us over the years. They got a lot of enjoyment out of us doing this."

"Our first year here was a bit rough," Ley interrupted, reaching over and squeezing Jere's knee. "We lived in an old horse hovel that we converted into a lean-to, with a car hood to build the campfire on. It was in '74, the rainiest summer on record. We ended up building a small tree house so we could cook, eat, and be warm. We had to get a gas stove; it was impossible to start a fire. In October, we moved into this part of the house, but it wasn't insulated, so we banked it with pine boughs. It would snow two or three feet at a time. It was so cold, we slept in layers of clothing and blankets. The cat would wake us up to start the stove. Finally, at Christmas, we ran out of wood and money, and had to stage a tactical retreat. But we promised ourselves we'd come back in the spring. So we went back to Massachusetts, got part-time work, and returned in May."

"I'm going to have the kids get cleaned up for lunch," Jere said. "Why don't you take Charlie down and show him the sawmill? We'll have some peanut-butter-and-jelly sandwiches when you get back."

The sawmill was down on the tree line, a quarter-mile from the house. Wild raspberry bushes dominated the field and surrounded the mill. Inside the sawmill, saw blades, peaveys, bucksaws, chains, pulp hooks, and various other logging tools hung on the walls. The mill was built like a lean-to, open on one side, with a small L-shaped room on the upper end.

"This is the engine room," Ley said, pulling back the curtain. "That's a Volkswagen motor; it runs the whole mill. It hasn't run for twelve years now, since we built the last section of the house. There really isn't much to see here. The carriage track's nothing but a piece of angle iron welded upside-down."

"I think it's quite an ingenious operation," I said, sitting on one of the tracks. "Where did you learn to do this?"

"Books. I read a lot. And my brother helped with the design and assembly. We had it set up in a week, but he spent the summer helping me refine it. I'll start it up again when I add onto the house. Hey, that's Jere hollering. Let's head up. She'll have sandwiches waiting — besides, the blackflies are beginning to find us."

Jere had lifted a basin full of hot water off the woodstove and was setting it in the sink when we walked through the door. The kids were sitting quietly at the table. "There you go, guys," she said. "While you're washing up, I'll go pump more water so I can be heating it for the dishes. Be careful of the kerosene lamp on the table. I lit it so it wouldn't be so dark while the sun's hiding behind those heavy old rain clouds."

"It must be difficult trying to read and teach the kids by kerosene," I said.

"We hook lights up to the generator sometimes," Jere answered, before going out the door. "But mostly we do everything the old way. About the only modern thing we have is a seventy-two-foot artesian well with a hand pump sitting on top. There's no electric pump. I even did my laundry by hand for years, diapers and all, until the kids started wearing jeans — they're too hard to wash by hand. Now Ley's mom, bless her soul, sends money to one of the laundromats in Houlton for us. When the laundromat gets low on money, they send her a note and she sends them more money. It's wonderful."

(A busy kitchen -- note the hand pump.)

Scrubbing his hands, Ley said, "We bathe using this basin."

"No privacy?"

"Well, we all stay in the other room when someone is bathing."

"The skunk came in once while I was taking a bath," Moira said, excitedly. "I was standing there washing and I felt something furry rub against my leg. Boy, did I scream!

Dad came running and said, 'Oh, it's just the skunk, he won't bother you.' Now we're all used to him. He comes in to get table scraps. Sometimes when we put the dishes down, he'll clean them off for us."

"You don't worry about him spraying you?" I asked, amazed.

"No," Ley said, handing me the soap, "he doesn't bother us. He's like one of the family now."

"How does he get in?" I asked, chuckling at Moira's excitement.

"Over here," Ramon said, jumping up from the table and pointing to a corner of the kitchen. "He comes right through that hole under the wall."

"Now, Ray, sit back down," Ley said, sitting down himself as Jere carried in two five-gallon buckets of water. She poured part of one into a kettle on the stove and put the rest on the floor. She sat down beside Ley and offered me two sandwiches and a glass of cold water.

"That's sweet water," Ley said. "You'll like it. It tastes like fresh spring water."

"When I had the babies, you didn't think it was so sweet, you had to lug so much."

"You had the kids here at home?" I asked.

"Yes, I guess we did," Jere said, putting her sandwich down. "Two of them were born at the hospital in Houlton, but the other two were born right here in this house. Ley was the midwife."

"No kidding," I said. "That must have been something. How did you like delivering babies?"

"It was extremely hectic," Ley replied. "Your first thought is, 'God, there's no way.' But you have to see it through. I ran around getting water, more water, and wood and kerosene. The good thing was she had short labors. And I pretty much knew what was going on. I learned by delivering goats."

"You learned by delivering goats!" I repeated, looking at Ley across the table. He was too serious not to be telling the truth.

"Yeah. Delivering goats isn't a whole lot different from delivering babies. If you can do one, you can do the other."

"You people do live the old way," I said. "You should write a book about your experiences, your life out here. You have some really incredible stories. I haven't run into anybody else who wines and dines skunks and learns how to deliver babies in the goat pen."

"Grandma came out to watch me when Krystl was born," Moira interrupted. "It's pretty cool telling people I have a brother and sister who were born at home."

"I bet it is," I replied, jelly oozing out of my sandwich.

"Yeah, she's quite proud of that," Jere said, handing me a paper towel. "But Todd can't say that. When we were expecting him, Ley's mom said, 'I'll come up and watch the kids if you'll go to the hospital. I couldn't live through that again. It's too hard on my blood pressure.' So she talked us into going to the hospital. But then Ley played midwife once again, when we had Ramon."

"You must have had some reservations," I said. "I mean, weren't you concerned about a possible problem developing? You're a long way from help."

"By gosh, she wasn't a bit nervous," Ley said. "I was, though. I felt isolated. If anything went wrong, there was nothing we could do. That would have been really hard to deal with. Actually, we did have a registered nurse from town. All she did was watch and then count fingers and toes.

She said, 'They're all here.' So, if we needed it, we did have that much help."

"Well, with or without a nurse, that's quite an accomplishment," I said. "When we were outside, you mentioned that Todd was in a program for talented youth."

"Yes, last year in the seventh grade they had to give Todd tenth-grade geometry and ninth-grade science. They all agreed that he's so advanced there was no use boring him. That's why he's at college now. Johns Hopkins University runs a special program in Amherst. We got a letter from him the other day. In two weeks, he's finished fifteen chapters of an eighteen-chapter text. He's always been way ahead of his age. He excelled right from the beginning. His letter was funny; he said, 'I've met some really strange, interesting, and brilliant people. I've also met one absolute nerd and an immature moron.' So we need to figure out what we're going to do with him. Intellectually, he's right up there, but emotionally, I don't think he's ready for college. People who are his emotional peers aren't his intellectual peers. Moira's the same way. She could have skipped grades and gone to college with Todd, but she chose not to. She was too eager to have the social experiences of her peers. We home school them until the sixth grade; then we let them go to public school if they choose. We believe in reincarnation. And I believe the kids chose this family because we would home school them."

"Tell me something, will you. You can't imagine how many people, when they find out the type of book I'm writing, say, 'It's too bad the kids have to grow up that way. They don't have a chance to get adjusted to society.' I've interviewed several couples with four or five kids and found just the opposite to be true. All the kids seem to be more advanced emotionally and scholastically than other kids their age, and well adjusted to society. There's a family not too far from here whose kids are so far advanced that they are used by the public school system as academic, problematic, and sometimes suicidal counselors. Why is that? Or am I just biased or naive?"

"We'll let Moira answer that," Ley said.

"It's all in values," Moira said, without hesitation, "and not just kids' values, but parents'. When I come home from school, Mom is always here. I don't come home to a babysitter, like a lot of kids. Being home-schooled helped, too. You can learn a lot on a one-to-one basis. A lot of kids at school think I'm lucky 'cause Mom is always home. Some kids go out and get in trouble just for attention. I get all the attention I need right here, and it's the right kind of attention. Mom even meets us at the school bus and we walk in together. We don't have the influence of television either. Don't get me wrong, there's nothing wrong with TV; it's *what* you watch. We don't have a TV, but we do things as a family. We go to church together, we go skiing. Dad helps me write. At night he reads to us. When Christmas comes, he reads stories about Christianity."

"The problem," Jere said, "is not with our kids being maladjusted, it's with the other kids. People are so blind. All they have to do is look around. How many of their kids are in trouble? But that's not the important question. *Why* are they in trouble? I think Moira answered that. But society can't see it. They think their kids have to have everything. Well, you can't buy love; it has to come from the heart."

Ley said, "Schools need to get back to the basics. We taught our kids the basics. Without bragging, they're so far ahead of the other kids that the teachers hate to see them leave their classes. And they can't wait for our next kid to get there."

"You folks should go to Washington and teach your values there," I said. "Tell me, just to change the subject a bit, what's been the biggest surprise you've had to deal with coming here?"

"Black flies! There's no doubt about that; they were the biggest shock," Jere answered. "We wrapped up like beekeepers and bathed in garlic, but nothing worked. We just ended up itching. The Indians used to go to the coast during black fly season. We obviously can't do that. But now that the yard is cleaned up, the flies aren't so bad. Even if they were, we have no desire to leave, none whatsoever. And when the kids are grown, we'll be just as happy to stay here. We'll do those things we always say we'll do when we have more time, like riding horses, my garden — there are lots of projects."

"And I have my books to write," Ley added.

Standing outside the doorway, I took photos of everyone but Ley. He said he was camera-shy.

In those final moments with the Armens, Moira spoke again and her final two words struck me. Speaking with love and conviction, her eyes brimming with tears, she said, "No matter where I go, I'll always visit often, real often. *It's home.*"

●●●●●

Ley died of cancer on July 17, 1993. He was forty-six. I visited Jere again shortly after Ley's death.

"We moved out here next to the road so it would be easier for the children to get to their school functions. It wasn't too long after the move that Ley died. I wonder if he just let himself get sick. He always had his heart set on living in the woods. His power spots were in the woods."

Looking at Jere across the table, I said, "On my last visit, you said Ley was a man of power. Now you speak of his power spots. Do you mind explaining that?"

"You'll probably think I'm crazy," Jere answered.

"I don't think so," I said. "I've been to three of Tom Brown's classes. He's America's most respected outdoorsman, and he speaks of 'the spirit-that-moves-in-all-things.'"

"I know who Tom Brown is. If you've been to his school, I'm sure you can understand. Ley communicated with that same spirit you learned about in Mr. Brown's classes. By concentrating on an object in front of him, Ley once leapt thirty feet from a crouching position on snowshoes. I saw him do it."

Leaning into the table, Jere continued, her expression stoic. "I think this is why we met, Charlie. Even if you don't admit or accept it," she said with deliberation, "you must understand that it was this same spirit who led you to all the people you are writing about — including us. Perhaps your writing talent will help other people understand. Have you read *The Quest* by Tom Brown?"

"Yes."

"Then let me remind you of part of the introduction," Jere said. She went into the living room and returned with the book. Sitting across from me again, she read:

"This book is a journey, a journey of flesh and spirit, from the world of purity of wilderness to that which is impure, distorted, and destructive; the world of modern society . . . It is difficult for anyone who loves wilderness to come back to the world of society, and it is the toughest path a man or woman can walk . . . But if we are to realize our

Vision and bring it to society, we must live within society."[3]

Jere paused, and then said with sincerity, "I believe this is, in large part, what your book is all about, Charlie. On more than one level, *it's home.*"

•••••

And Jere Armen was right.

---

[3] Tom Brown, Jr., *The Quest* (New York: Berkley Books, 1991), pp. 3-5.

(Armen Family Study Room.)

(The woodshed at Jere Armen's.)

(Flagstaff Lake)

Epilogue

Many people have asked why I trekked all over the state looking for people who live in the wilds of Maine. In reply, I note all that would be missing from my life if I had not done so. Each visit was instructive:

- Fun-loving Aime Lecours, who lived in a cabin on Holeb Pond, passed away a couple of years after I visited him. I believe he was 92. I learned a great lesson from Aime. He said, "I'm too old to care what happens anymore; I just enjoy today."
- Outgoing Butch and Rachelle Hunt, from Roque Bluffs up Machias way, just from observing them, taught me to relax and listen to the quiet whisperings of the spirit. I haven't seen them in years.
- Creep City, a village of great people, welcomed me, treated me like their own, and fed me a turkey dinner at the village social. They still live life to its fullest.
- Rose, a quiet Native American, who moved from New York City to Grand Isle "to get away from it all," taught me how to live life in the slow lane.
- An outgoing trapper, John Latwin, who lived in the mountains above Coburn Gore, is still roaming the mountains. He was not just at peace in his surroundings; he was happy.
- A guide with a great sense of humor, Chub Foster, who lived with his smiling wife, Fran, in a cozy home on the backside of Grand Lake Mattagamon, reminded me of the Waltons without the kids. They didn't need any; they

were the kids. The Fosters have both passed away. When I left them, I knew that I needed to find the kid in me once again.

- Fun-loving David and Janet Cormier lived on the side of a mountain and enjoyed every bit of it. It saddens me to know that Janet passed away at a very young age with cancer. David is still roaming the hills and hiking the Appalachian Trail. They were a close couple. Their love for each other was so evident that it bubbled over like a boiling teakettle. After visiting them, I knew that I needed to find a mate who understood me, and I her, as they understood each other.

- Bert and Maggie McBurnie, and Oscar Gagnon, were grinning storytellers from Chesuncook. They were comical folks with a backwoods wit. Oscar and Bert have passed away. Maggie, after selling their lakeside cabins, still visits the old homestead during the summer months. From their wit and laughter, I rediscovered some of mine.

- Jim Quinnam, a stern man from Waldoboro, was as straight-laced as his ugly black and white collie. I hope the collie has died. Jim still grows tall, beautiful plants in his garden. He is a man who doesn't care what he says, or who hears him say it. I tried not to learn anything from Jim; his garden was different than mine.

- Some real earth-loving, back-to-the-landers, Ley and Jere Armen from Linneus, with all their kids and critters, had a spirit about them that I have found to be unmatched anywhere. Ley died from cancer at a young age. After we had talked most of the day, Jere said to me, "We met for a reason. I think you needed to find yourself, and I think you now finally have." She was right.

These are people who are *Bound by a Common Thread*. They have chosen a humble life style. They work enough to take care of their needs and don't worry about what others have. They stay home and take part in their children's lives. They're more than moms and dads to their kids; they're friends. They're perfectly focused in their choices to raise their families off the grid. They enjoy quality one-on-one family time. They grow a garden together, and for the most part the kids don't complain, because their interest is piqued from mom and dad teaching them about each plant, wrestling with them in the grass, and having water fights. They respect, grow, and love their animals together while learning about each animal and its purposes. Most often, each child raises his or her own lamb, cow, goat, chicken, or whatever. They help in birthing, which helps them learn about reproduction in a respectful way.

One person, when he found out what I was doing, commented, "I wouldn't raise my kids that way. They wouldn't be socially adjusted."

"Mister," I said, "you owe it to yourself to visit some of them. And when you do, you'll come away with a different attitude."

I interviewed over thirty families during the course of this project. Without exception, it was easy to see the happiness in each of the children. If they were feeding the sheep, they were also hugging and kissing them. If they were slopping the hogs, they were also riding them. In the garden, they could tell you what each plant was, its uses, and even if there was a plant out of place. Mother, daughter, and son would work in the garden together, smile, hug each other, and mom would take the time to teach each child more about the plants.

By the time the children reached junior high, they were given the opportunity to attend the regular school system if they so chose. By that time they could read better, write better, spell better, and do math better than many college students. And there wasn't much about history they didn't know. They were the most respectful, well-educated kids I have ever met. Some chose to attend the regular school system and some chose to attend every other year. In every case, the teachers praised the kids and the parents. They said, "Send us more kids like this." Some of the kids were so advanced that they skipped over whole school years to the next grade level. Some high school sophomores attended John Hopkins University programs for talented youth. Others chose not to attend schools for talented youth, but rather opted to stay with their friends in high school. Some were asked to tutor other students. Some were asked to be counselors to other students. At least one was asked to be a counselor of suicidal students.

So, I ask, "Who is socially adjusted and who is not?"

Certainly their way of life is different and sometimes less convenient, depending on your point of view. They would argue that convenience lies in how you look at it, and they would be right. Their way of life is only chosen by a few, but that number seems to be growing as more and more people get tired of the everyday hustle and bustle of today's society, and choose the convenience of an alternative lifestyle.

Some would say these people are too isolated. However, in most cases they can get out to a nearby town in an hour or less. It takes me over an hour to drive from Millinocket to Bangor. It's true that I have local stores. It's also true that these people have a good supply of food and other needs on hand, and they're not running around in a blizzard shopping for snow blowers, shovels, etc. Instead, they're sitting by a fire enjoying popcorn, telling stories, reading, playing games as a family, napping, or feeding the friendly skunk.

The kids in these families will always remember the good times, the times with their animals, the times in the gardens, the times wrestling with mom and dad, and the times eating popcorn around a cozy fire while a nor'easter blows, drifting snow up to their windows. Most will someday return and pensively, with tears dripping down their cheeks, visit the old homestead, listen to the echoes of the past, and forever be *Bound by a Common Thread*.

About the Author

Charlie Reitze, a native Mainer, graduated from Bonny Eagle High School in Standish, Maine, in May of 1967. In July of 1967, he joined the Army and served a three-year stint. He served in the 62nd Engineer Battalion in Vietnam from September of 1968 to September of 1969. After being honorably discharged in 1970, he worked in the construction field for most of his work-a-day life.

In 1990 Charlie started a course of study at The University of Maine at Farmington. He graduated in 1994 with a Bachelor of Fine Arts in creative writing. He also is a graduate of Tom Brown's Wilderness Survival School, and Solo Wilderness First Aid and CPR. He wrote a survival column for *The Northwoods Sporting Journal* from 1993 to 2016. He has also hiked several portions of the Appalachian Trail and was an AT volunteer maintainer.

Today he is retired and loves to spend time relaxing and fishing at the family camp in Eustis and several other fishing spots. And he loves to tell stories!

(Charlie at the Maine Troop Greeters Display, Bangor Airport)